Get Them Thinking!

Use Media Literacy to Prepare Students for State Assessments

Sue Lockwood Summers

Linworth

PUBLISHING, INC

**Your Trusted
Library-to-Classroom Connection.
Books, Magazines, and Online.**

DEDICATION

This book is lovingly dedicated to Bob - my husband, partner, editor, mentor, coach, support system, encourager, and best friend!

Library of Congress Cataloging-in-Publication Data

Summers, Sue Lockwood.
  Get them thinking! : use media literacy to prepare students for state assessments / Sue Lockwood Summers.
       p. cm.
  Includes bibliographical references.
  ISBN 1-58683-172-0 (pbk.)
  1. Audio-visual education. 2. Media literacy. 3. Critical thinking—Study and teaching. 4. Educational tests and measurements—United States. I. Title.
LB1043.S89 2005
371.33'5—dc22

2004012670

Author: Sue Lockwood Summers

Linworth Books:
Carol Simpson, Editorial Director
Judi Repman, Associate Editor

Published by Linworth Publishing, Inc.
480 East Wilson Bridge Road, Suite L
Worthington, Ohio 43085

5 4 3 2

TABLE OF CONTENTS

TABLE OF FIGURES, REPRODUCABLES, and TRANSPARENCIES

INTRODUCTION

Twenty years ago I was a teacher and a single mother. For professional as well as personal reasons I became interested in learning about the effects of the mass media on children. At that time there was a great deal of research and professional writing about television and its effects on children. I decided to pursue a Master's degree in this area, but discovered that the media courses were basically "how-to" classes, such as how to create slide-tape presentations, how to use a darkroom to develop film, and how to write computer programs. Even after I received a Master's degree in Media, I continued to learn all I could on the subject of the mass media's ability to shape and influence the lives of children and teenagers.

I had the privilege of meeting an intriguing and wonderful man who taught graduate classes. He convinced me that I should take the information I had learned and offer a course for teachers. He turned out to be a very influential man in my life (he is now my husband) and he helped me design and develop a graduate course entitled "The Effects of Mass Media on Children." I taught this class for the University of Northern Colorado. After a few years, I realized that the course centered on the issues and problems, but did not offer helpful and hopeful solutions for teachers and parents.

In 1991 I stumbled upon the term "media literacy" and quickly discovered that it referred to critical thinking about the messages of the media. I took a professional sabbatical from my media specialist position and attended seminars and meetings, including a conference in Canada on the topic of media literacy. Much to my surprise there were hundreds of people in attendance from all over the world; they were from Scotland, England, New Zealand, Australia, France, and numerous other countries. There were relatively few people from the United States. I attended workshops and keynote presentations and connected with people in the United States group. The conference was life-changing.

By the time I returned to Colorado I was convinced that media literacy was the solution to many problems that had been attributed to the mass media. The United States is the foremost producer of media in the world, but at that time only a handful of teachers in the United States were infusing media literacy techniques into their teaching.

I created another graduate class with the assistance of my husband and began offering the course, "Media Literacy: How to Teach Students to Be Critical Thinkers About the Mass Media." Since then I have presented media literacy strategies at parent-teacher nights, teacher in-services, and educational conferences. I authored *MEDIA ALERT! 200 Activities to Create Media-Savvy Kids* (MEDIA ALERT! 2000) and co-authored *Changing the World through Media Education* (Fulcrum Publishing, 1998).

At the 2002 conference of the Colorado Educational Media Association, one of many conferences that has allowed me to share my passion for media literacy, I described my strategies for using media literacy to prepare students for state assessments. Donna Miller, editor for Linworth Publishing, was in the audience and asked me to write a book on this topic for media specialists and teachers.

The impact of state assessments on teachers and their daily curriculum choices has been phenomenal, and the ramifications of these standardized tests seem endless. One significant result is the limit placed upon "extra" curriculum units because they are not specifically detailed on the tests.

As a library media specialist in an elementary school for more than 20 years, I have seen teachers bring their own styles and interests to their classroom settings. Some might be fond of drama and allow the students to create and act out skits. Others have a passion for science and their classrooms are filled with realia from nature. Still others are travelers and encourage students to "visit" foreign places throughout the school year.

However, as accountability has tightened for teachers, administrators, and school boards regarding students' test scores, those teacher-developed extras have vanished and the rigors of the "3 Rs" have once again assumed a position of dominance.

For thirteen years I have been an advocate of media literacy—the application of critical thinking to the messages of the mass media. During that time teachers and students have shown a genuine interest in learning about the creation, development, distribution, and impact of media messages on individuals and on society. Media literacy stimulates us to be better consumers and better citizens. We could not have a democracy without the media because most of what we know about government and society comes from information delivered via the mass media. On the other hand, it is imperative that the media know that the consumers of their messages demand truth and responsible reporting.

In years of teaching graduate courses in media literacy and speaking at educational conferences, I have never met anyone who does not believe that critical thinking is an essential part of what students need to learn. However, media literacy does not appear as a specific section on most state assessments, so teachers have had to let the subject matter slide or wait to teach it after the tests are over.

In reality, media literacy is part of the tests, as all state assessments do in fact measure the critical thinking of students. Media literacy teaches students about the culture's messages in order for them to become wiser and more savvy about the world around them. What could be more crucial than authentic critical thinking?

During the years I have taught lessons that integrate concepts of media literacy into existing courses for students of all ages, I've observed that:

- students are highly motivated to learn about the media,
- teachers readily accept this approach as a necessary ingredient of a complete education, and
- communities that are properly introduced to this topic realize that the schools are broadening the education of their students.

After these experiences, in which media literacy training enabled students to perform better as test-takers and as citizens, I wrote this book. In schools across the nation it is essential to merge into extant curricula opportunities for students to practice critical thinking to prepare for state assessments and for life.

Three things make this book unique and worthy of the readers' time.

- Collaboration is highlighted. Media specialists can cooperate with content specialists and will find curriculum tie-ins for the activities in this book, despite the vast amount of curriculum content classroom teachers at all levels are required to cover every day.
- Integration is the key. No media specialist or teacher has extra time in the teaching day for additional subjects, so media literacy must be merged into the existing school day.
- Lessons in this book are authentic, meaningful, and interesting. Students enjoy analysis, investigation, and creation of media messages and will look forward to media literacy lessons.

Chapter 1 is an introduction to the topic of media literacy for media specialists and teachers. For some, media literacy is a new subject area, while others may be familiar with it but have decided it was not feasible within existing time constraints. State assessments are currently a major issue in education across the nation and will be with us for the long term, but we must teach students what they need to know, not merely how to pass tests. Integration of media literacy into existing curriculum is proposed throughout this book as a cure for the state assessment blues.

In each of the next five chapters one aspect of the media process is discussed. Lessons for students in elementary school, middle school, and high school are offered. Each lesson has a curriculum tie-in and consists of authentic media-related activities for the students. The topics in this book are related to state assessment content focusing on the teaching of proficiencies students will need to succeed. A quick look at the Table of Contents shows the skills that regularly appear on state assessments, such as summarize, predict, sequence, determine point of view, target audience, format, writing styles, use appropriate word choice, analyze poetry, draw conclusions, and interpret statistics.

Chapters 1 through 8 contain helpful, ready-to-use reproducibles that supply a structure for gathering information and writing responses. In addition, a number of transparency masters are included. There is a glossary of terms and definitions. The Appendix lists articles, books, Web sites, videos, and other resources to extend learning beyond the specific lessons described in this book.

For the activities in this book, media specialists and teachers can determine the specific media to be utilized and the amount of time to allocate for each lesson. Specified media and instructions for activities are merely suggestions, as educators regularly modify lessons to fit the needs of their students.

Go ahead and highlight text, write notes in the margins, add ideas for the next time the lesson is taught and personalize these lesson plans. This is a book to be used, not just read and stored on a shelf.

Teachers, media specialists, and students will never read, hear, or view the media the same way again after involvement with the activities in this book. They will become actively engaged in the process of analysis and want to discuss their impressions with others. Their eyes and ears will become more aware of the media's messages and their excitement about the culture will be infectious. Students will benefit from this dynamic approach, and school administrators may wonder why the test scores are better than ever before.

As teachers and media specialists integrate study about the current culture into daily lessons, media literacy will no longer be considered a new or superfluous subject, but the most effective way to teach critical thinking.

CHAPTER ONE

OVERVIEW

State assessment tests are inevitable in schools across the United States. Standardized assessments have been adopted as a form of accountability to measure the degree of learning that is taking place in our nation's schools. The accountability is justified because the nation's citizens who indirectly pay for the education system require it. State standards have been set in place, and they direct the development of the school curricula, which are, by definition, dynamic. Curricula must be modified periodically to keep up with contemporary ideas and strategies.

In addition to their function of measuring student learning, state assessments have also been used to gauge levels of teaching in the schools and, consequently, the performance of each school. This additional application of state assessment tests has introduced underlying questions of validity because the tests have been developed to measure achievement of students and their results are commonly used to rate effectiveness of teachers.

It is general knowledge within the education community that state assessment scores do not necessarily reflect the high level of teaching and the dedication of educators in most schools. Teachers are often frustrated with their students' test scores, knowing that assessment topics have been adequately covered prior to the tests. It is apparent that low test scores do not necessarily correlate with the educators' level of expertise in their fields. One ramification of state assessments is that teachers refocus on teaching specific skills and knowledge. They continue to attend workshops, graduate classes, and conferences to learn better methods of teaching reading, writing, mathematics, and other subjects. Instruction does not seem to be at fault.

If there is an appropriate and well-planned curriculum and educators are hard at work preparing and sharing lessons on specific test topics, why do state assessments not mirror this excellence? It appears that students do not individually digest and transfer all that is taught to them during the school year. How can test scores better reflect the overall quality of teaching that occurs in classrooms during the school year?

The concern of teachers and media specialists is not what to teach. There is actually more curriculum to cover than time allows. The solution, therefore, must be to make changes in teaching strategies. It is essential that educators take a different approach. To continue to teach in a manner that does not effectively impact student performance on state assessments perpetuates the status quo. A different, more successful approach to teaching requires consideration of critical thinking aand media literacy.

Critical Thinking

One constant on all state assessments is critical thinking. Educators must integrate critical thinking into all curricula to generate a lasting impact, rather than merely focusing on facts and skills within the subject matter. Teachers who recognize the goal of teaching thinking rather than just imparting knowledge help students make connections beyond the content of the coursework. However, due to pressure to complete the curriculum content within the confines of the schedule, attention is usually focused on the school curriculum.

For instance, as teachers create lesson plans about various writing styles, they usually draw on samples from library books or texts that are available within the school. They might have students use critical thinking lessons, such as "compare and contrast the two writing styles in these two essays." This activity will develop critical thinking. However, this lesson overlooks the opportunity to extend the learning to writing styles that are available outside of the school and part of the daily lives of students. A surefire way for critical thinking training to permeate all lessons is through the use of media literacy strategies.

Media Literacy?

Media literacy refers to the skills and knowledge needed to question, analyze, interpret, and evaluate media messages. It is the application of critical thinking to the messages of mass media that saturate our culture. A simple definition, created by the Alliance for a Media Literate America, states:

> Media literacy empowers people to be both critical thinkers and creative producers of an increasingly wide range of messages using image, language, and sound. It is the skillful application of literacy skills to media and technology messages. As communication technologies transform society, they impact our understanding of ourselves, our communities, and our diverse cultures, making media literacy an essential life skill for the 21st century (www.amlainfo.org/medialit/index.php).

Four steps to media literacy are awareness, analysis, reflection, and action.

- Awareness   The first step to becoming media literate is an increased awareness of the messages of the media. An example of a lesson to accomplish this step is for students to list as many types of print and electronic media as they can. The outcome of the lesson is that students take notice of the communication methods that are being utilized in the culture around them.

What Is Media Literacy?
A Broader Definition

"Within North America, media literacy is seen to consist of a series of communication competencies, including the ability to ACCESS, ANALYZE, EVALUATE and COMMUNICATE information in a variety of forms including both print and non-print messages. Interdisciplinary by nature, media literacy represents a necessary, inevitable, and realistic response to the complex, ever-changing electronic environment and communication cornucopia that surrounds us.

To become a successful student, responsible citizen, productive worker, or competent and conscientious consumer, an individual needs to develop expertise with the increasingly sophisticated information and entertainment media that address us on a multi-sensory level, affecting the way we think, feel and behave.

Today's information and entertainment technologies communicate to us through a powerful combination of words, images and sounds. As such we need to develop a wider set of literacy skills helping us to both comprehend the messages we receive, and to effectively utilize these tools to design and distribute our own messages. Being literate in a media age requires critical thinking skills, which empower us as we make decisions, whether in the classroom, the living room, the workplace, the boardroom or the voting booth.

Finally, while media literacy does raise critical questions about the impact of media and technology, it is not an anti-media movement. Rather, it represents a coalition of concerned individuals and organizations, including educators, faith-based groups, health care-providers, and citizen and consumer groups, who seek a more enlightened way of understanding our media environment."

Used with permission from the Alliance for a Media Literate America (AMLA), <www.amlainfo.org/medialit.html>

- Analysis   This step involves "deconstruction" or the investigation of all parts of a message, such as the text, image, background, and props. At this level students should recognize that media messages did not just happen but that each was carefully designed.
- Reflection   At this point the viewer, listener, or reader identifies the opinions, attitudes, and beliefs within the message and compares them to his own ideas. A suggestion for a lesson at this level is to assign students to visit a Web site and reflect on ideas that are presented.
- Action   This final step focuses on what will be done with the message. Perhaps the message causes anger and instigates a letter-writing campaign. Perhaps it is a reminder of the speed limit and causes the driver to slow down. An activity that gets to this level involves students' completing the first three levels and then taking action, such as writing a letter to the editor of a newspaper about a topic that has captured their interest.

It is important to note that media literate citizens must reach all four levels, but students may not attain all levels at each grade level. Educators must consider the four steps and have students reach the levels that are appropriate in each lesson.

Media literacy can be found in the state standards of almost all states, although the term "media literacy" might not actually be used. For example, the Colorado Content Standards for Reading and Writing include:

Standard 2: Students write and speak for a variety of purposes and audiences.

Standard 4: Students apply thinking skills to their reading, writing, speaking, listening, and viewing.

Standard 5: Students read to locate, select, and make use of relevant information from a variety of media, references, and technological sources.

The state's content standards acknowledge the wide range of skills that must be mastered in the education process. In addition, Information Literacy Standards state that the student who can access, evaluate, and use information critically and creatively and contributes in a positive and ethical way is information literate.

What About That Test?

When teachers and media specialists extend learning beyond the classroom and initiate opportunities for students to think critically about the media messages that fill today's culture, students are motivated to retain the skills and knowledge in a new and personal way. The transfer of learned skills to new situations is thus

National and State Standards

The driving force behind all curriculum development and test preparation is a set of content standards written by and for each state. Following is a list of Web sites to use in locating sets of national standards and compilations of state standards. Readers should also check specific state and school district standards.

State-by-State Media Literacy Standards (within content standards)
<www.med.sc.edu:1081/statelit.htm>

McREL National Standards and Benchmarks Compendium
<www.mcrel.org/compendium/browse.asp>

McREL National Media Standards
<http://198.17.205.11/compendium/Benchmark.asp?SubjectID=7&StandardID=10>

Colorado Information Literacy Standards
<www.cde.state.co.us/cdelib/slinfolitindex.htm>

AASL Information Literacy Standards
<www.ala.org/Content/NavigationMenu/AASL/Professional_Tools10/Information_Power/Information_Literacy_Standards_for_Student_Learning.htm>

National Standards for History
<www.sscnet.ucla.edu/nchs/standards>

National Standards for Civics and Government
<www.civiced.org/stds.html>

National Science Standards
<www.nap.edu/readingroom/books/nses/html>

Standards for the English/Language Arts
<www.ncte.org/about/over/standards/110846.htm>

Curriculum Standards for Social Studies
<www.ncss.org/standards/toc.html>

Math National Standards
<http://standards.nctm.org/document/index.htm>

National Geography Standards
<www.nationalgeographic.com/resources/ngo/education/standardslist.html>

National Educational Technology Standards
<http://cnets.iste.org/students>

National Standards for Music Education
<www.menc.org/publication/books/standards.htm>

National Standards for Arts Education
<http://artsedge.kennedy-center.org/teach/standardss.cfm>

Physical Education Standards
<www.mcrel.org/compendium/Standard.asp?SubjectID=18>

improved. Each test presents unique and never-before-seen problems and writing samples in which students must use their prior learning to comprehend, decipher, and apply their knowledge and skills. For example, students may have read many stories during the school year and followed their teachers' instructions to determine the authors' purposes for the writings. When a new piece of writing is offered on the test, teachers assume previous experiences will enable students to remember and then transfer the skills from the prior lessons. However, the content and format of the test item might be radically different from the stories that students have experienced. This assessment is truly a test of the students' broader critical thinking skills, rather than a specific skill to determine an author's purpose.

Educators who teach critical thinking rather than a series of individual skills will enable students to handle any test item. Critical thinking is often seen as obtuse and unwieldy for teaching in a classroom. However, by using media literacy strategies, critical thinking activities that are focused on media messages, teachers connect with their students' lives in a meaningful way and teach critical thinking concepts that will stay with students.

The goal of media literacy is not to create cynics. There exists a continuum of thinkers, with sponges on one end and cynics on the other.

Continuum of Thinking

Sponges ———————— Healthy Skeptics ———————— Cynics

Sponges absorb everything they see, hear, or read and assume all of it is true. Cynics dismiss everything they see, hear, or read and assume all of it is incorrect or biased information. The media literate citizen must be a healthy skeptic with skills to judge the reliability of sources of information, to verify the validity of facts, and finally to reflect on the meaning and impact on one's personal life. However, these skills are not innate; they must be learned and practiced.

Figure 1.3, on page 6, is the *GrassRoots Taxonomy of Thinking Skills* (adapted in Canada from Bloom's Taxonomy) gives a visual breakdown of levels, verbs that best reflect thinking at each level, and examples of each. The *GrassRoots Taxonomy of Thinking Skills* can be a valuable aid when media specialists and teachers create lessons.

Critical thinking skills in this book are generic to all state assessments. Many critical thinking skills can be taught or reinforced by applying them to messages of the mass media.

Integration and Collaboration

The keys to successful media literacy lessons are integration and collaboration. No teacher has time to teach extra subjects. Therefore, media literacy cannot be handled as a separate subject.

The integration of media literacy education into existing curriculum areas encourages students to look at the world around them in new ways, perhaps for the first time, while they study the curriculum content. The teacher or media specialist

GrassRoots Taxonomy of Thinking Skills

(adapted from Bloom's Taxonomy of Thinking Skills)

Category	Knowledge Information Gathering	Comprehension Confirming	Application Making Use of Knowledge	Analysis (Higher Order) Taking Apart	Synthesis (Higher Order) Putting Together	Evaluation (Higher Order) Judging the Outcome
Description The skills demonstrated at this level are those of:	• observation and recall of infor- mation; • knowledge of dates, events, places; • knowledge of major ideas; • mastery of subject matter.	• understanding information; • grasping meaning; • translating knowledge into new context; • interpreting facts, comparing, contrasting; • ordering, grouping, inferring causes; • predicting consequences.	• using information; • using methods, concepts, theories in new situations; • solving problems using required skills or knowledge.	• seeing patterns; • organization of parts; • recognition of hidden meanings; • identification of components.	• using old ideas to create new ones; • generalizing from given facts; • relating knowledge from several areas; • predicting, drawing conclusions.	• comparing and discriminating between ideas; • assessing value of theories, presentations; • making choices based on reasoned argument; • verifying value of evidence; • recognizing subjectivity.
What the Student Does	Student recalls or recognizes information, ideas, and principles in the approximate form in which they were learned.	Student translates, comprehends, or interprets information based on prior learning.	Student selects, transfers, and uses data and principles to complete a problem or task.	Student distinguishes, classifies, and relates the assumptions, hypotheses, evidence, or structure of a statement or question.	Student originates, integrates, and combines ideas into a product, plan, or proposal that is new to him or her.	Student appraises, assesses, or critiques on a basis of specific standards and criteria.
Sample Trigger Words	• define • list • label • name • identify • repeat • who • what • when • where • tell • describe • collect • examine • tabulate • quote	• predict • associate • estimate • differentiate • summarize • describe • interpret • discuss • extend • compare • contrast • distinguish • explain • paraphrase • illustrate	• apply • demonstrate • complete • illustrate • show • examine • modify • relate • change • classify • experiment • discover • use • compute • solve • construct • calculate	• separate • order • explain • connect • divide • compare • select • explain • infer • arrange • classify • analyze • categorize • compare • contrast • separate	• combine • integrate • rearrange • substitute • plan • create • design • invent • what if? • prepare • generalize • compose • modify • hypothesize • develop • formulate • rewrite	• decide • grade • test • measure • recommend • judge • explain • compare • summarize • assess • critique • justify • discriminate • support • convince • conclude • select • rank • predict • argue
Sample Task(s)	Name the food groups and at least two items of food in each group. Make an acrostic poem about healthy food.	Write a simple menu for breakfast, lunch or dinner using the food guide chart.	What would you ask shoppers in a supermarket if you were doing a survey of what food they eat? (10 questions)	Prepare a report about what the people in this class eat for breakfast.	Create a song and dance to sell bananas.	Make a booklet about 10 important eating habits that would be suitable for the whole school to follow in order to eat correctly.

needs to present the subject matter that is to be taught in an innovative way.

Collaboration between the media specialist and the classroom teacher or specialist teacher can reap huge rewards. The library is not an entity unto itself but is a service center catering to the needs of the entire school. Students often do not see connections between what is learned in the library media center, what is learned in the classroom, and what is necessary for success in the "real world." Effective collaboration can result in significantly more realistic and exciting lessons for students. Information skills taught in the library and applied to the subject being studied in the classroom work best when the teacher and media specialist have planned the lessons together and perhaps even taught them together. Each of these specialists brings experience and knowledge to the team. Media literacy can become part of each lesson plan to ensure that lessons are authentic and that they focus on real-life examples. This innovative technique, the integration of media literacy strategies, motivates students to see the "bigger picture" without resulting in a curriculum that is overloaded with additional instructional units.

This book is filled with lessons that can be used in the collaboration process. Consider specialist teachers as well as the classroom teachers. Perhaps there is a gifted-and-talented class or a special-education class, where the teachers rarely work directly with the media specialist. Perhaps there has been ongoing collaboration between the classroom teachers and the media specialist, but the art, music, and physical education teachers have never felt the need to work together. The concepts of media literacy might initiate new and compelling reasons for collaboration.

An excellent way to collaborate and to bring the world into the classroom is the use of classroom sets of newspapers. The format and content of this medium can provide dynamic topics for study. News articles, advertising, and opinion pieces offer valid writing styles to analyze.

Newspapers in Education

Many local and regional newspaper organizations now have "Newspapers in Education" departments. One function of the department is to participate in the educational process by offering multiple copies of newspapers delivered to the school and bundled for classroom use. The papers are offered at reduced rates and in some instances, as a result of local sponsorships, are free to teachers.

The use of classroom sets of newspapers offers numerous advantages to K-12 teachers and media specialists and is beneficial to almost every curriculum area. Teacher guides are related to individual subjects and current news sections or topics. Some offer teacher guides with strategies to help students prepare for state assessments.

Teachers and media specialists have found newspapers invaluable in teaching about current events, photojournalism, "hard" news, "soft" news, advertising, layout, bylines, editorials, reviews, headlines, comic strips, inserts, coupons, travel, history, sports, the stock market, geography, math, language arts, English, drama, writing styles, and many more subjects. Contact a local or regional newspaper to learn about the guides and services available to teachers.

Cable in the Classroom

Cable in the Classroom is the cable industry's nonprofit education foundation. Its purpose is to connect educators with programming and resources that have been designed and distributed via cable channels with students in mind. Check out the Web site at <ciconline.org> for a dynamic source of information about learning resources, advances in teaching and learning, and demonstrations of the educational power of broadband technology. *Access Learning* (formerly known as *Cable in the Classroom Magazine*) is provided to schools by local cable companies throughout the nation. The magazine lists curriculum-related programming in subject areas and offers a monthly overview called "Taping Highlights." In addition, the magazine has timely articles, "Content Connections," "Web Spotlights," "Teacher Tips," and other sections which are helpful for media specialists, teachers, and administrators. It also offers contact information for education-friendly cable networks. Below is a list of network Web sites to enable educators to learn more about teachers' guides and curricula that are available, most of which are free.

Web sites for popular cable network resources include:

A&E Network	<www.aetv.com/class>
Biography Channel	<www.aetv.com/class>
BRAVO	<www.bravotv.com/>
Cable News Network (CNN)	<www.cnnstudentnews.com>
Discovery Channel	<http://discoveryschool.com>
The History Channel	<www.historychannel.com/classroom>
Home & Garden Television	<www.HGTV.com>
Nickelodeon Channel	<www.teachers.nick.com>
WAM!	<www.wamtv.com>

Many teachers and media specialists are leery of introducing television programming into their school days, believing that students see far too much television outside of school. In reality, television networks offer many instructional and educational programs that enhance learning by bringing school subjects to life. Most educators are familiar with the benefits of public broadcasting programs, and cable provides opportunities to collaborate with claassroom teachers.

Five Essential Questions

This book is unique in that it applies the focus of critical thinking to five essential media literacy questions. Each of the five questions is the focus of a chapter in this book, and each chapter includes grade-appropriate lessons for students in elementary, middle, and high school. The questions cause students to investigate the content and format of media messages, the role of mass media in our culture, and the impact of those messages on themselves and on society. This process breaks the topic of media literacy into manageable questions that can be asked about all media messages. These questions supply the outline for learning activities in this book.

Five essential questions that supply the framework for this book are:

Who created the message? (Chapter 2)

The focus is on the author or creator of the message; the purpose the creator had in mind; the point of view, and perhaps bias, in the message; the author's intended audience for the message; and the format the author selected.

What is the message? (Chapter 3)

At this point, analysis (deconstruction) of the message begins. Through close examination the reader, listener, or viewer concentrates on the parts that make up the whole. Thinking skills include investigation of writing style, word choice, and image; determination of whether the message is fact or opinion, fiction or nonfiction; the ability to summarize content and put it in sequence; and the recognition of statistics and how they can influence us.

How was the message delivered? (Chapter 4)

The focus of activities and discussion is on context and visual clues, genre, how messages capture the attention of the audience, and poetry as a style of communication.

What is the impact of the message on me? (Chapter 5)

This chapter concentrates on reflection, where the focus is on personal reactions and responses. Skills to be developed here are essential in activities such as judging the reliability of the message and recognizing personal responsibilities.

What is the impact of the message on society? (Chapter 6)

The last question in this series is concerned with the ability to draw conclusions, make inferences, predict, and judge the worth of a message. These are higher-level thinking skills that enable students to look beyond their own lives and critique the media's roles in society. Each student continues to further develop an individual "hierarchy of believability."

Chapter 7 provides instruction and learning activities to help students move to the next step, the creation of original media messages. At this point students have covered the five essential questions and completed the four steps of media literacy. Now the fun begins! Students work at a higher level of Bloom's Taxonomy of Thinking because they are functioning at the synthesis level. They get excited as they realize it is time to create, design, develop, compose, invent, or rewrite, and let their creative juices fly.

In **Chapter 8** support is offered to expand the integration of media literacy into all curricula at every level. Additional activities are supplied to help media specialists and teachers work together to merge media literacy into the daily lives of students. As media literacy becomes an integral part of all subject areas, students will become critical thinkers and better citizens.

There is a **Glossary** of terms, some of which may be new to readers. The **Appendix** is an assortment of resources that includes media literacy organizations, lesson plans, books, Web sites, and videotapes.

Media Literacy and Student Learning

Numerous studies have attempted to assess the impact of media literacy training on students. One recent study, "Measuring the acquisition of media literacy skills," in the July/August/September 2003 edition of *Reading Research Quarterly*, was developed by Renee Hobbs and Richard Frost. Hobbs, one of the founders of the media literacy movement in the United States, currently teaches at Temple University in Pennsylvania.

> This research examined one central question: How does media literacy instruction, integrated within a yearlong course in high school English language arts, affect the development of students' message comprehension, writing, and critical thinking skills? ...
>
> This study measured students' comprehension and message-analysis skills in response to three nonfiction message formats: reading a print news-magazine article, listening to a U.S. National Public Radio (NPR) audio news commentary, and viewing a television news segment targeted at teenagers. Comprehension skills were measured after exposure to each message through a paper-and-pencil response to open-ended questions. Writing skills were measured by coding a sample of open-ended response text for word count, holistic writing quality, and the number of spelling and usage errors. Analysis skills were measured after exposure to each message with use of paper-and-pencil measures with open-ended and checklist items to determine students' ability to identify purpose, target audience, construction techniques, values and point of view, omitted information, and comparison-contrast...
>
> This research shows that media literacy instruction embedded in a secondary-level English language arts course can be effective in meeting traditional academic goals...
>
> This study shows how specific textual-analysis skills can be acquired through classroom activities that incorporate a variety of types of popular media.

The study acknowledged a definite improvement in learning as compared to the control group.

How to Start

To change the school design or the approach that teachers use in school cannot be accomplished by one person. It is necessary to start the discussion about media literacy and see who is ready to get involved. Then a study group can be formed. The process should grow and generate the interest of other educators. Individual media specialists, curriculum planners, and teachers can begin media literacy strategies in their media centers and classrooms with support from the administration. However, impacting the entire school or district will require time and resources and should be considered at least a two-year process.

Perhaps as the students discuss, investigate, examine, and judge media messages during their learning activities, the media specialists, teachers, and support staff will also be challenged to question, analyze, interpret, and evaluate the media messages that fill our culture. Not only will the students welcome the new approach that focuses on the world around them, but also many of the conversations in the hallways, on buses, in homes, and in the community will be critiques of the mass media.

State assessment scores should slowly improve without major changes in funding, class size, or radical shifts in programs. Media literacy is that powerful.

Getting the School Administration Involved

Gaining the school administration's support is the first step in the process of integrating media literacy into the school's curriculum. Before media literacy is merged into the daily lives of students, it is important for those people who will be directly involved to have conversations with the principal, assistant principal, and perhaps the area superintendent, depending on the size of the school district. During the discussions it will be wise to share copies of the state-by-state media literacy grid, found at <www.med.sc.edu:1081/statelit.htm>. The grid details how media literacy language is merged into each state's content standards in areas such as language arts, social studies, and technology.

It is important to be prepared to present and explain information about media literacy, including what it is, how it will benefit students, and, most important, how this approach is likely to enhance scores on state assessments. It may be prudent to bring samples of media literacy lesson plans and resources to meetings with the administration. Chapter 8 discusses more thoroughly the concerns about paring back school activities in order to improve student performance on tests. It would be advisable to absorb that material before the meeting in order to better field concerns about whether media literacy is extraneous to the curriculum.

Gaining the cooperation and support of the administration should be seen as a process, not a stand-alone effort. Since the focus is to modify all curricula at all grade levels, it is important that sufficient background information be made available. Locate articles about media literacy in education journals and share copies with administrators prior to the first meeting. Use the resources found in the Appendix to locate media literacy articles. The more the teachers and media specialists have done their homework regarding the benefits of media literacy, the more likely media literacy will be embraced as a positive innovation.

Once the administration is "on board," offer in-service training to teachers to whet their appetites about media literacy, share easy-to-use lesson plans such as those found in this book, and generate discussions about the mass media, not as a threat to existing curriculum, but as an approach that bridges the gap between school and the rest of the culture and improves state assessment results.

Getting the Community Involved

In addition to the school administration, the community of parents also needs to be introduced to this approach. Students should not suddenly be studying television commercials or magazine covers without their parents being involved in the media literacy process and the reasons for the change in the curriculum. Until the term "media literacy" becomes a household term, it will need some explanation.

A presentation to the school board to offset concerns might be a fruitful first step. Then the parent-teacher organization at the school might arrange for a Media

Literacy Night for parents and family members. On page 13, the Reproducible 1.1, "Parent Letter" offers a sample letter that, with local modification, can be sent to families before the Media Literacy Night to generate interest. Transparency 1.1 "How Is Media Literacy Related to State Assessments?" also found in this chapter on page 14, offers topics for discussion with teachers, school board, parents, and other interested community members. It is not necessary to cover all media literacy activities that are to be incorporated. It is important that parents have an introduction to the topic and an opportunity to participate in sample media literacy activities and discuss prospective benefits from the new approach.

(School Letterhead)

(Date)

Dear Parents,

In an age when the mass media have become part of all of our lives, it is essential that the study of mass media messages be part of your student's education. As a means of preparing students for state assessments and successful lives, we have decided to integrate media literacy into the curriculum at our school.

Media literacy is the application of critical thinking to the messages of the mass media. The skills and knowledge in this field of study prepare students to question, analyze, interpret, and evaluate the messages they see, hear, and read. The critical thinking that will be part of learning in all subject areas will help students become discerning and competent citizens. Media literacy may be a new term, but critical thinking has always been part of education.

We invite you to be part of the education process. We are scheduling a MEDIA LITERACY NIGHT to be held at the school on (date)_____ (time) _____. Please plan to attend and learn more about this motivating approach to learning.

We look forward to seeing you at the meeting.

Sincerely,

Consider these critical thinking skills that are included on state assessments and are also inherent in evaluating media messages:

- Discriminate Between Fact and Opinion
- Determine Point of View
- Recognize the Author's Purpose
- Classify as Fiction or Nonfiction
- Summarize
- Identify Genre
- Recognize the Writing Style
- Interpret
- Compare and Contrast
- Judge the Reliability
- Analyze
- Develop Organizational Skills
- Improve Vocabulary
- Predict What Happens Next
- Determine Relevance
- Sequence
- Draw Conclusions

CHAPTER TWO

WHO CREATED THE MESSAGE?

The first step in analyzing any media message, print or electronic, is to identify the author or creator of that message. There is a very specific reason for the creation of each message. The message's originator had a built-in purpose and point of view (POV) and also determined who the target audience would be for the message. Finally, the author selected a specific format for the distribution of that message.

As students learn to dissect a message in order to determine the purpose, point of view, possible bias, target audience, and selected format, they will be more able to think about why the message was created.

Media messages surround us all day long. These messages can be seen or heard on ads, signs, magazines, newspapers, television, radio, billboards, clothing, and innumerable other sources. The newest and perhaps most intriguing messages come via the Internet, which does not follow the rules of traditional media.

Though we refer to these media messages in total as the "mass media," they are all results of efforts by humans who wrote, composed, illustrated, or designed each message. Furthermore, in traditional media, there was most likely a "gatekeeper" who was the decision maker, determining whether each message was appropriate, correct, acceptable, and ready for distribution. Examples of gatekeepers are the editor of the newspaper, news director at the television or radio station, boss at the advertising agency, producer of the television program or movie, and manager of a political campaign. Each individual is also a gatekeeper when he makes decisions about what information to share with children, a spouse, colleagues, and friends.

Whether the message is a magazine ad for a dandruff shampoo, a public service announcement (PSA) urging the audience not to drink and drive, or a television commercial for a presidential candidate, there was someone who decided on the specific content to be included and the precise format to be utilized. Focusing on that author can give us insights about the message.

Author

It is easy to identify the author of a book. Publishers follow prescribed guidelines for book covers and title pages. Look at the title page of this book, Figure 2.1, and it is easy to recognize the title, author, and publisher.

Figure 2.1: Title Page of This Book

Get Them Thinking!

Use Media Literacy to Prepare Students for State Assessments

Sue Lockwood Summers

Linworth
PUBLISHING, INC

Your Trusted
Library-to-Classroom Connection.
Books, Magazines, and Online.

In magazines and reference materials the authors of articles may or may not be given credit. Messages found on flyers, posters, catalogs, clothing, television commercials, signs, radio announcements, and in other similar mass media rarely list the author of the message and refer only to the company or organization that has paid for the production and distribution of the message. The identity of the author or creator of an Internet media message might also be difficult to detect.

Purpose

The purpose is the reason for the message. The originator had a definite goal in mind. Whether the message is a personal e-mail to a family member, a billboard for people traveling on a major highway, or a political cartoon for an organization's newsletter, there is always a reason for the production and distribution of the message. The purpose may be commercial, informational, or educational in nature. Our daily lives are bombarded by literally thousands of commercial messages, making it hard to realize that media makers can have a wide assortment of non-commercial motives. The goal of most messages is to inspire us to buy something, do something, go somewhere or, at the very least, to produce brand allegiance. A public service announcement (PSA) is an example of a message that is created for a different purpose—to educate or to advise the public.

In addition to the myriad of media messages that have obvious purposes, there is another category which contains subtle or nebulous messages. Some of them, such as the "drink responsibly" ads from alcohol manufacturers, carry within the message a sense of altruism.

How to Determine the Author of a Web Site

The URL extensions in the Web site address can offer a great deal about the site's author or creator, and perhaps the primary purpose for the site. Keep in mind that these are merely guidelines, not rules, and there are exceptions.

Consider these URL extensions:

.com	commercial; sponsored by a for-profit organization or company
.net	sponsored by an organization or company that operates an internet network
.org	sponsored by a non-profit organization
.edu	sponsored by a college, university, or other school
.us, .ca, etc.	resides in a particular country (us = United States, ca = Canada); state and local governments use this extension
.gov	sponsored by an agency of the United States government or a state government
.mil	sponsored by the United States military

(Used with permission from *The Web-Savvy Student: Ten Media Literacy Activities to Help Students Use the Internet Wisely*, by Betsy Hedberg, published by Curriculum Adventures, 2001, <www.studentactivities.com>.)

Sometimes recognizing the author or creator of a Web site is more difficult than merely reading the URL endings. Alan November's excellent book, *Empowering Students With Technology*, explains how to "look deeper" to determine the originator of a Web site. Most Internet users are stumped in trying to identify authors of Web sites, but the following progression makes the task rather straightforward:

- Copy the address (URL) of the site.
- Go to <www.alltheweb.com> and place the URL in the search bar.
- Decode the Web site information.
- Use the "who owns this site" link to investigate the owner or creator of the Web site.

Alan November states, "It's easier to be manipulated if you don't know the rules." His book also shows media specialists and teachers how to use the "forward links" and the "external links" to learn even more about a Web site.

Visit Alan November's Web site at <www.anovember.com> to learn more about his resources and conferences for educators.

Point of View

The point of view (POV) of the author or creator determines the choice of words, the format, the style or layout, and the impact of the message. In fact, the point of view colors all aspects of the message. The point of view is the opinion of the author, although the message may be delivered as if it were strictly factual. It is certainly human to have opinions so it is not surprising that the media maker has some embedded in the message. Sometimes the point of view is obvious; other times it is subtle or even invisible.

Although it may be expected that the media maker has a point of view, the presence of bias is generally not anticipated. Bias is different in that it is an unfair preference for, or dislike of, something or someone. It is more insidious than an opinion and can alter information or present it in a prejudicial manner. Bias is having a set opinion or idea and keeping it in a logic-tight compartment so as not to see new information in a new way. Consider the following continuum to clarify the relationship between fact, point of view, and bias:

Fact ——————————— POV ——————————— Bias

It is essential that students be capable of detecting bias so as to not be persuaded by it, and be able to distinguish a point of view from fact.

Target Audience

Not all messages are meant for all consumers or all citizens. Suppose the candidate for mayor of Chicago has hired an excellent campaign organization, which has created a poignant and powerful 30-second television commercial to promote their candidate. If that ad is aired only during Saturday morning cartoon programming in the Baltimore, Maryland, area, it will not do the candidate much good with Chicago voters, the target audience, because they will not see the ad. A great deal of time and attention goes into research through market analysis and demographic surveys to define the intended audience and determine how best to influence them. The rise of focus groups over the past 20 years shows that advertisers are learning how to intentionally pinpoint specific target groups. The more the advertiser knows his audience's reactions, preferences and needs, the better he can customize the ad for that audience.

This focus on determining the target audience is not merely for the world of advertising, however. The news industry—in all of the various formats—uses these same strategies to determine their audience. When we examine our present society, we realize that we are practically saturated with news stories from various media. The news is literally the only industry that starts each day with nothing and must turn it into a "something." Every other industry works on yesterday's problems, plans, and priorities, but by definition the news must be "new" each day.

"What to select" becomes the driving force in the news business. With unlimited sources of news stories, the gatekeepers must constantly be decision-makers: which stories to include, which story will be "the lead," which stories to ignore, and which ones will need accompanying visuals. A major factor in the gatekeepers' selections is which stories will stimulate the readers, listeners, or viewers to patronize their news outlets each day.

There are two ongoing considerations for gatekeepers at each news source: news that the people need to know and news that the people want to know. Most news agencies attempt to offer a balance of these two types of stories.

Format

The choice of format can make a significant difference in the impact of a message. Consider, for instance, the best reason possible for reading books. Now suppose that reason (the content) is placed on a sign in Times Square, but printed using a font that is so small that people cannot read it as they pass by. Although the message is important, no one is influenced by it because the format is not appropriate. Selecting the correct format is an integral part of the creation of an effective message. Media makers spend a substantial amount of money, time, and effort to determine the best format for their messages. Sometimes one message will be presented in various formats, such as cigarette ads that are found in magazines and newspapers and also on billboards. This is done to saturate the market with recognizable icons, images, or slogans, thus insuring immediate name recognition by customers or voters. Suppose a favorite cereal were advertised only in words, with no pictures. How would that impact the consumer? The format is a key consideration in the development of a media message.

Students need to become "investigative reporters" eager to seek out the individual, group, or organization that decided the message was important enough to spend time, effort, and money to produce and distribute. They must question the content and format of the message and evaluate the reasons the message was created or selected.

At all levels students can be given opportunities to look deeper and think critically about the creators of media messages. Media analysis initially requires students to: determine the creator, the purpose, the point of view, the intended audience of the message, and the rationale for the selected format. Armed with these skills, all consumers (educators, students, and other community members) can investigate the motivation behind media messages. This is "step one" in the process of media literacy.

On state assessments, the test components often include wording such as:

- determine the author's purpose
- draw conclusions about the author's point of view
- identify the audience the author had in mind
- infer the author's feelings or attitudes about the topic
- justify the format the author selected

After involvement in the activities in this chapter, the students will be better prepared to correctly answer these test questions. A meaningful way to begin this study of the media is to distribute copies of Reproducible 2.1, "My Media Diet" found on page 27. This assignment will cause students to become aware of the media in their lives and trigger discussions about the messages that saturate the culture.

ACTIVITIES

Note: All directions in the "Activities" section of each chapter are written for teachers and media specialists. "Assignment" and "Discussion" sections are worded for students.

Author

Curriculum Tie-in: Information Literacy

Elementary School

- Use library books to review the information that is usually found on the title page: title, author, illustrator, and publisher.
- Review the difference between an author, illustrator, and publisher.
- Select and distribute library books that contain information about the author. Have each student read the facts about an author and share what was learned.
- Explain that not all books give information about the author. Ask where they might be able to learn more about the author of a book, such as reference books or searching the Internet to locate the publisher's or the author's Web site.
- Ask why it is important to know information about the author.
- Assignment: Select a favorite author, locate the publisher's or author's Web site, and write down five facts about your favorite author.
- Allow students to share what they learned about their favorite authors.
- Each time students read books during the school year, have them include information about the author with their book reports.

Middle School

- Discuss why it is important to know information about the author or creator of a media message or written piece of literature.
- Introduce the information offered on page 17 in Figure 2.2, "How to Determine the Author of a Web Site," regarding various URL endings and the further investigation of a Web site's creator.
- Select a topic that is related to their current curriculum for the students to research.
- Request students do an Internet search on this topic and locate and compile a list of Web sites that have different URL endings.
- Have them visit five of those Web sites and attempt to determine the author or creator of the sites.
- Assign students to visit the Web site: <www.comics.com> and select their favorite comic strip.
- Direct them to click on the "about the author" link to learn about the artist who created the comic strip.
- Lead a discussion about how knowing the identity of the originator

of a Web site helps the Internet user know whether the site is reliable, appropriate, or usable.

<u>High School</u>

- Locate an age-appropriate brief documentary film (current or historical). Use the Cable in the Classroom listings online, <www.ciconline.com>, or read the monthly *Access Learning: Cable's Guide to Education Resources* magazine to learn about documentaries offered via television.
- Discuss documentaries and how they are different from movies.
- Show the documentary to the class and have students react to the film by writing their observations and thoughts.
- Have students use the Internet to attempt to learn more about the media maker who created this documentary and the topic that was discussed. Have students learn what background the originator has regarding this subject. (Hint: If the documentary was aired via television, visit the Web site of the network that aired it.)
- Allow students to share their findings with their classmates.
- Ask students to give specific examples of other documentaries that seem to reflect the opinions and attitudes of their originators. Concentrate on how important it is to know about the author of any media message.

Purpose
Curriculum Tie-in: Language Arts and English
<u>Elementary</u>

- Define the word "purpose." Explain that every author inevitably has a reason or purpose for writing.
- Give students copies of Reproducible 2.2 found on page 28, "The Perfect Setting," and read it aloud to the class.
- Discuss ideas regarding the author's purpose for writing this piece.
- Assignment: Select a topic that is personally important. Write a persuasive paragraph that is meant to convince others about the ideas expressed.
- Have each student then read aloud the paragraph while the other students attempt to recognize the author's purpose for writing.
- Each time students read (or hear read aloud) written work, take time to discuss the author's purpose.

<u>Middle School</u>

- Collect a variety of magazines.
- Display the covers of the magazines.
- Discussion: What do all the covers have in common? What are some

differences?

- Have students work in small groups with five or more magazine covers. They are to discuss the purpose of both the content and the format of each of the magazine covers.
- Instruct each student to select one of the magazine covers and share some ideas with the class.
- Explain that there is never anything on any cover that is accidental and that every aspect of every magazine cover has been chosen, discussed, and agreed upon.
- Discussion: What is the purpose of magazine covers?
- Help students make a large display with the magazine covers. They must then decide on a catchy statement to place on the display, such as, "Every part of these covers was designed with a purpose!" Position the display where other students will see it, such as in the cafeteria or hallway.

High School

- Discuss political campaign ads.
- Show a video of a 30-second televised campaign ad for a political candidate (current or historical).
- Discussion: What facts were in the ad about the actual platform or intentions of the candidate?
- Discussion: What is the purpose of a 30-second campaign ad? How is a television campaign ad like any other television commercial?
- Repeat this discussion activity with other videotaped campaign ads.
- Have each small group of students create a fictional political character and then produce a 30-second ad attempting to sway the voters to vote for this character. Videotape the ads.
- Show each ad to the rest of the class (and other classes, if time allows). Discuss the real purpose of each ad.
- Assign students to write an essay comparing or contrasting a specific campaign ad with an ad for a well-known commercial product.

Point of View (POV)
Curriculum Tie-in: Language Arts and English
Elementary

- Ask the students to explain the difference between a fact and an opinion. They can use the dictionary to learn more about these words.
- Direct students to tell the class about their favorite candy bars. After everyone has had a turn, ask, "Did everyone have the same answer? Why not?" Talk about opinions and how they are different from facts.
- Define the phrase, "point of view," and explain that this is like the

word "opinion." Explain that authors and media makers have their own opinions, or points of view, and that their points of view can often be recognized in their messages.

- Give each student a copy of Reproducible 2.2, "The Perfect Setting," found on page 28, to read or read it aloud to the class. Ask students to determine the author's point of view.
- Each time students read or hear selections of writing, take time to discuss the author's point of view.

Middle School

- Bring to class a variety of bumper stickers.
- Ask students to discuss why people put bumper stickers on their vehicles.
- Explain that bumper stickers are slogans, capsulated ideas, or brief opinions and are actually premises, not arguments. Have students look up these words in a dictionary and write down the definitions.
- Assignment: During the next week write down the content of all of the bumper stickers you see and bring the list to school.
- Have each student select five of these bumper stickers and write a paragraph about each one, summarizing the bumper sticker's point of view.
- Instruct students to share one of their written bumper sticker summaries with the class. Discuss other possible points of view for each one.

High School

- Collect a variety of newspaper editorials. Create enlarged transparencies of these editorials to use with the class.
- Discuss the purpose of an editorial.
- Review the term "point of view." Start each class session reading one of the editorials aloud and have students react to the opinions expressed.
- Assignment: During the next week collect and read five newspaper or magazine editorials. For each editorial, summarize the point of view of the author. Submit the editorials and the summaries to the instructor.
- Discuss other media messages that are obvious reflections of the point of view of the author or creator.

Target Audience
Curriculum Tie-in: Language Arts and English
Elementary

- Introduce the term "target audience." Explain that all writers and other media makers have a specific target audience in mind for their messages.

- Have students discuss the kind of television commercials they have seen while watching cartoon shows.
- Assignment: Watch a television program and write down the names of all of the products advertised in the television commercials during that one program.
- During the next class session, ask each student to tell the name of the television program he watched, one product that was advertised during that television program, and possible reasons the sponsor selected that particular program for the advertisement.
- Each time the students read or hear selections of writing or watch a video, take time to discuss the author's intended audience.

Middle School

- Collect alcohol product ads from a variety of magazines. Tape each ad to construction paper.
- Introduce the term "target audience." Explain that all writers and media makers have a specific target audience in mind for their work.
- Allow students to work in small groups. Give each group five or more alcohol product ads. Have them determine the target audience for each ad. Then they select one ad and share their opinions about the intended target audience for that ad.
- Ask each student to select one of the ads and create an original ad for the same product intended for a different target audience.
- Discussion: Why is it important for advertisers to select a specific target audience for their message?

High School

- Review the term "target audience." Explain that all writers and media makers have a specific target audience in mind for their work.
- Have students use the Internet to visit four Web sites of well-known companies or entertainment media. Hand out copies of Reproducible 2.3, "Who Is the Target Audience?" found on page 29. As they visit each Web site, they are to list the name of the company or product, the Web site address (URL), and their ideas about the target audiences. They need to give specific reasons for their determinations.
- Discussion: Did the Web site's content and format match the target audience? Justify all answers.
- Have each student write an e-mail message to one of the companies with an evaluation of its Web site, including whether it was appropriate for the target audience.

Format

Curriculum Tie-in: Information Literacy

<u>Elementary</u>

- Define the words "media" and "format."
- Help students suggest as many types of media formats for messages as they can and compile their answers on butcher paper or a white board.
- Give students a list of sample reference questions, such as:
    Who named the Pacific Ocean?
    Who won the World Series in 2001?
    What is the telephone number of the local public library?
- Have them work in small groups to determine the right references (formats) they would use to find the answers.
- Discussion: Why are some formats better for some types of information?
- Ask students to bring in messages in different print formats: such as magazines, newspapers, bumper stickers, or flyers. Have the students examine the different types of messages in the various formats.
- Discussion: Why are some formats better than others for selected messages, such as an ad for peanut butter, a lost puppy announcement, or movie theater listings?
- Have each student select one of the messages brought to the class. Ask him or her to share the message with the class and justify or refute the use of that particular format for the selected message.

<u>Middle School</u>

- Ask what the word "analyze" means. Choose a student to look up the definition in a dictionary and read it to the class.
- Introduce the "4 Part Analysis." (Reproducible 2.4 located on page 30)
- Review the terms: content, format, intent (or purpose), and personal reaction.
- Give each student a copy of Reproducible 2.4.
- Assignment: Select one medium and one message (for example, television and a specific commercial or a "sitcom"), read, view, or listen to the selection, and complete the analysis worksheet.
- During the next class session, talk about the results of the assignment. Discuss why people can have different personal reactions to the same message delivered by the same medium.
- Use this analysis reproducible often when students are required to analyze a media message.

<u>High School</u>

- Review these terms: media, content, and format.
- Discuss what happens if the content of a message is maintained but

the format is altered. Have students give examples.

- Assign each student to bring a print advertisement to the next class session.
- Instruct students to study their ads and then create new ads:
    - keep the same format but change the content
    - keep the same content but change the format
- Have the students share their new ads with the rest of the class.
- Discuss the difference between content and format and the importance of selecting the right format for specific content.
- Invite someone from the advertising industry to the class and allow students to question him or her about the content, format, and impact of ads.

Name _____

Date _____

The mass media have become a part of our lifestyles. From the time we wake up (to a clock radio?), to the time we go to sleep (to a CD playing?), we are involved with media messages.

Use this paper to record all of the media messages you are exposed to during one day. Include listening to the radio in the car or bus, noticing signs or billboards, viewing videos in classes, and even reading the messages on people's clothing. Then answer the questions.

Date of media diet study: _____
_____
_____

Morning: _____
_____
_____

Afternoon: _____
_____
_____

Evening: _____
_____
_____

Which medium is the most important in your life? _____
_____
_____

Why? _____
_____
_____
_____

Which medium would you be willing to live without? _____
_____
_____

Why? _____
_____
_____
_____

It was my favorite time of the day. The sun was just beginning to set and the sky was filled with puffy cumulous clouds. The reflected vibrant colors made me smile. It occurred to me that a summer sunset in Colorado is just too spectacular to describe in words. As I watched the sun set, I looked around at the meadow and thought I saw movement out of the corner of my eye. I was hoping an elk or perhaps a family of deer would decide to wander through the field, to nibble at the grass and enjoy the peace of the evening. Whatever it was stayed in the covering that the trees provided.

I had been following the news stories. News of a developer who planned to bring stores to this area filled the local papers each day. Editorials were written and people's conversations all seemed to gravitate to this worrisome topic. How could anyone consider changing the natural environment of this perfect setting? There were already plenty of stores nearby. There were stores for clothing, food, auto parts, video rentals, ice cream, and numerous other items. There were buildings filled with offices for insurance salesmen, real estate brokers, bankers, doctors and dentists. Why did they need this meadow?

The trees were still and the woods were dark as I continued to ponder this situation. The colors were gone now, but it was still light enough to see the gray tones of twilight. Darkness would soon overtake the meadow and the nocturnal animals would begin their rituals. It was time for me to leave.

As I carefully walked along the rocky trail, I glanced back at the meadow one more time. It was hard to imagine what this area would look like next year when I visited again. By then the buildings would be finished and the stores would be teaming with shoppers. I knew I would hold this evening in my memories, forever remembering the beauty of this meadow.

Name _____

Date _____

Visit the Web sites of four companies and complete the chart.
(Give specific reasons for your target audiences.)

Company or product: _____
URL: _____
Target audience: _____
_____
_____
_____
_____

Company or product: _____
URL: _____
Target audience: _____
_____
_____
_____
_____

Company or product: _____
URL: _____
Target audience: _____
_____
_____
_____
_____

Company or product: _____
URL: _____
Target audience: _____
_____
_____
_____
_____

Name _____

Date _____

Format   Content

Intent (Purpose)   Personal Reaction

CHAPTER THREE

WHAT IS THE MESSAGE?

It is time to look closely at the media message. While it is important for students to study the message's creator, purpose, point of view, target audience, and format, as well as other issues concerning the development of each message, the message itself must be closely analyzed. The topics listed in this chapter are all components of the analysis process. Teaching students to analyze can be difficult. When teachers ask students to "analyze" a message, the results can be a mixture of responses. The word "analysis" is confusing and hard to explain. When teachers demonstrate exact strategies students need, use straightforward words they understand, and offer repeated practice opportunities, students are able to develop skills in analysis.

Deconstruct the Message

Media literacy embraces some terms that might be new. The reader, listener, or viewer must learn to "deconstruct" or take apart the message to examine all of the message's components in order to comprehend it. This is a practical application of the process of analysis.

For example, if the message takes the form of a magazine ad, the student will study the various elements such as background, props, the product being advertised, animals or people in the ad, layout, text, colors, tone, target audience, their personal reactions, and the overall impact. As students study each of these parts there is an understanding that everything in the ad is intentional. No longer can ads merely wash over the reader; there is now a method of analysis to be applied to every ad.

A starting place for the examination of media messages might be to copy and distribute Reproducible 3.1, "Icons, Slogans, and Jingles" found on page 46. This worksheet will trigger involvement with messages that have become part of the media landscape. Students often do not realize that each icon, slogan, and jingle was carefully created, written, or designed, and should be recognized as the end product of a great deal of time and effort. This assignment will raise the awareness of students and stimulate discussion about the messages they see, hear, or read.

Writing Styles

In print media, the writing style of each piece can help determine the impact of the message. It is important to review the various writing styles that are traditionally studied in language arts and English classes. Writing styles include: fictional narrative, research, narrative, expository, persuasive, reflective, biographical, editorial, and letter writing. The lessons in this chapter use actual examples of the various writing styles commonly used in messages of the media. Lessons on writing styles using authentic contemporary writing are motivating, and students' learning can readily transfer to other messages outside of the school setting. The more genuine samples of writing that students learn to identify, the better equipped they become to recognize and deal with these writing styles wherever they occur.

Critical thinking about the media's messages might include a lesson on bumper stickers, for example. During this study it is important to reinforce the idea that any argument that can fit on a bumper sticker is not in reality an argument at all—it is a premise. The distinction is noteworthy. An argument implies an exchange of ideas with substantial information; a premise is just one person's assertion. The students have been bombarded by premises in their culture—on bumper stickers, billboards, and T-shirts, in slogans and campaign ads—to the point where premises might be mistaken for rational reasoning. The next step can be to introduce essay writing. There must be factual support, not just personal opinions, offered in an essay. Essays require extensive research and the defense of ideas. A follow-up assignment would be to have students write essays to expand their thinking beyond the simple slogans and premises they see everyday.

Word Choice

An author who uses the right words can make the text sing, sting, come alive, excite, enlighten, frighten, or amuse. Word choice can make or break the written work. Students who recognize the importance of proper vocabulary choices become better readers and better writers. In fact they will quite frequently be judged by their vocabulary. Assessment tests require an extensive knowledge of vocabulary, an understanding of how the words utilized by an author can sway or influence the reader, and some aptitude for various types of writing. The activities in this section stimulate students to evaluate word choice in different media settings in order to improve their own reading and writing.

Images

In our visually-saturated culture, images and their effects are crucial and consequently must be studied. There are endless choices of images available to the media maker. The Internet, for example, has sites with drawings, photographs, animations, videos, and illustrations. The image used in a message is selected with great care and with a specific goal in mind and is never a haphazard choice.

It is important for students to realize that the actual images of recognizable models, celebrities, candidates, and other individuals in photographs found in newspapers, magazines, music videos, Web sites, and movies are most likely altered. The ability to fix, modify, and eradicate images is available to all, thanks to computers, scanners, and image manipulation software. Students must be aware of the reasons for images in media messages, as well as the effects these images have on viewers and readers. One manifestation of image manipulation can be seen in the photos on popular magazine covers. It is common practice to touch up, redo, and even manufacture images for the covers without legal or moral consequence. Photographs can no longer be considered as evidence of truth or reality, due to the ease with which they can be altered. The selection, purpose, and impact of images used in media messages require all of us to be ever wary so as not to succumb to their influence.

Fact vs. Opinion

It is essential to know whether a message contains facts or opinions. That judgment is becoming more difficult due to the merger of these types of writing. An example of this fusion occurs in newspapers. In times past, opinions were relegated to the editorial pages of newspapers. Now it is common practice to integrate opinions into the writing elsewhere in the paper, even the hard news stories. When students learn to substantiate facts and recognize opinions, they are empowered to read and discern, not merely for a test, but in other situations throughout their lives.

Fiction or Nonfiction

Media specialists regularly teach students the differences between the content of the fiction and nonfiction sections of the library. Though students may be able to explain differences between fiction and nonfiction books, they might not be able to recognize those distinctions in media messages or on test questions. Each piece of writing was created to be either fiction or nonfiction. That decision drives the development of the writing, including such aspects as the purpose, style, format, vocabulary, length, and illustrations. Students must be able to determine whether the piece was meant to be informative or entertaining. Students need to scrutinize a message and quickly determine whether it is real or made up.

Summary

Students at all levels must learn to summarize a media message, either orally or in writing. Summaries can be found in many real life situations, such as the television listings that provide a synopsis of each television program. This skill is one that students will use throughout their lives and one that can be readily applied to many situations. The more students have opportunities to summarize, the more they develop the skill to comprehend and reword the essence of any message.

Sequence

Adults often take the sequence of ideas or events for granted, recognizing that there are stages in writing—the beginning, middle, and end of a story, for example. Students at all grade levels need to identify the order or sequence within each media message so they can think critically about the steps in the development of the piece. To make this skill a fundamental part of their lives, they need to be asked frequently about the sequence of events. This ability to put print or electronic messages in the proper sequence is basic to the comprehension of all messages.

The ability to motivate students to recognize writing styles, word choice, and other aspects of our language has been hampered by using writing examples that are not genuinely part of the students' lifestyles. The activities in this chapter present opportunities to teach various components of language arts by relating them to the mass media that saturate the culture and that students interact with several hours per day. Studying language elements by relating them to media messages plays right into students' hands due to their active attraction to the media. Media literacy is a breakthrough for those teachers who have struggled for years to find some practical and appealing application of the rather abstract subject of language.

In addition, reading and writing are major components of all state assessments. Students may find test sections that require them to:

- Summarize the story.
- Identify the writing style.
- Replace the underlined words with synonyms.
- Explain whether the piece is fiction or nonfiction; justify the response with specific illustrations.
- Circle the opinions in the writing.
- Sequence the statements in the same order in which they occurred in the story.
- Write an original piece in a specified writing style.

Statistics

The application of numbers within a message can affect its impact. Students must be willing and able to question and think critically about the use of numbers. Authentic examples of statistics encourage students to recognize and analyze the use of numbers in media messages, such as news, sports, and advertising. The media specialist and the math teacher can collaborate to ensure that the role of statistics is fully understood so that students don't merely accept data without researching the facts for themselves. Statistics can be powerful and persuasive and need to be investigated before being accepted.

The math state assessments measure students' abilities to read graphs, charts, tables, and other forms of math information. Students must also be able to solve word or story problems. The more real math is to students in their daily lives, the less it will seem like just a subject they study at school. The application of math concepts will be dramatic.

Media messages offer authentic opportunities for investigation and analysis. Each of the activities in this chapter will trigger higher-level thinking and develop healthy skeptics—and better test takers!

Math in the Media

Charts, graphs, tables, and statistics can be found in countless print, electronic, and Internet sources. When students learn to pause and consider the purpose and reliability of these numbers, they are thinking critically.

Numbers are part of our daily life: news, coupons, sales, advertisements, weather maps, stock information, television listings, recipes, election results, and sports statistics. Data and number facts fill the news media.

By subscribing to the local newspaper or an age-appropriate student news magazine, such as *Time for Kids*, students will soon recognize that math is part of news and part of their daily lives.

Frank Baker has created a teacher-friendly Web site, which offers practical lessons using math from actual news articles. It can be found at <http://medialit.med.sc.edu/mathinthemedia.htm>. The lessons are ready-to-use and feature authentic references to math in real life situations.

Watch for television programs that focus on math concepts and make math come to life for students. Refer to the current issue of *Access Learning* magazine (formerly known as *Cable in the Classroom*). Some examples of math programs include:

Elementary:	"Square One TV"
	"TLC Elementary School"
	"Cyberchase"
Middle School:	"Adventures of the Aftermath Crew"
	"Math Vantage"
High School:	"SportsFigures"
	"In the Mix: Financial Literacy: On the Money!"

ACTIVITIES

Deconstruct the Message

Curriculum Tie-in: Information Literacy

<u>Elementary</u>

- Have students bring empty cereal boxes to class for several weeks in advance of this lesson.
- Discuss the word "deconstruct" (to take apart and examine).
- Copy from page 47 Reproducible 3.2, "Components of a Media Message," and use it as an overhead transparency or student handout. Explain each component on the list.
- Hold up one cereal box and ask students to give their ideas about each of the listed components related to the images and words on the box (ignore those components that don't fit). For example, have them discuss the colors and background on the box.
- Have students work in small groups. Give each group a cereal box. Have the students use the checklist on Reproducible 3.2 to discuss the components of the cereal box. Have them share their ideas.
- Use other cereal boxes as time allows in order to deconstruct these media messages.

<u>Middle School</u>

- Ask students to bring magazine ads to the next class session.
- Copy from page 47 Reproducible 3.2, "Components of a Media Message," and use it as an overhead transparency or student handout. Explain each component on the checklist.
- Have the students work in small groups. Give each group one magazine ad. Ask students to discuss each component on the list and then share their ideas.
- Ask students to think about how changes to various components of the ad might impact the total impression. (For example, if the ad had used different props or a different background.)
- Each student then selects another ad, deconstructs it using the checklist, and writes a journal entry about his reaction to the ad and its various components.

<u>High School</u>

- Have students bring posters of famous rock stars, athletes, and other celebrities to the next class session. Place the posters on the wall.
- Review the word "deconstruct" (to take apart and examine).
- Copy from page 47 Reproducible 3.2, "Components of a Media Message," and use it as an overhead transparency. Discuss each

component on the list.

- Have students work in small groups and have each group deconstruct one celebrity poster on the wall.
- Discussion for each group: If you had created the poster, what component would you have changed?
- Allow time for each group to share their ideas with the class.

Writing Styles

Curriculum Tie-in: Language Arts and English
Elementary

- Review the many types of writing styles, such as narrative, reflective, persuasive, and expository.
- Have students locate and bring print examples of each writing style to the next class.
- Read aloud these authentic examples of writing styles and have students determine which writing style each piece is, based on the definitions that were discussed.
- Place the examples students have brought to class on bulletin boards or posters that have been displayed for each writing style.
- Refer to the displayed examples throughout the school year when discussing writing styles.

Middle School

- Collect editorials and letters to the editor from local, regional, or national newspapers.
- Discuss the persuasive style of writing.
- Have students read the editorials and letters and discuss them.
- Have each student select and research facts about a favorite topic. (For example, locate information about the video games rating system and facts in support or against the use of such ratings.)
- Have students write persuasive editorials or letters to the editor explaining their positions, including both facts and opinions.
- Have each student read aloud the persuasive writing piece. Have the class select the best one to submit to the local or school newspaper.

High School

- Discuss "reviews" as a type of persuasive writing.
- Have students find, read, and bring a written review of a book, movie, CD, restaurant, or video game to the next class.
- Have students write down at least three facts and three opinions from the review to submit to the teacher or media specialist.
- Assignment: Write a review of a book, movie, CD, restaurant, or video game.
- Have students share their reviews with the class.

Word Choice

Curriculum Tie-in: Language Arts and English
<u>Elementary</u>

- Subscribe to a weekly or biweekly age-appropriate news magazine for the students' use in class activities.
- Each time students read a news article, have them locate new vocabulary words in the article.
- Add the words to a vocabulary list on the wall and have students research and share the definitions.
- Ask why each new word was important to the article in which it was used.
- Draw attention to the displayed new vocabulary words. Have students try to use the words in their speaking or writing.
- Repeat this activity often throughout the school year as magazine articles are read.

<u>Middle School</u>

- Arrange to have students receive newspapers delivered to the school by the local paper's "Newspapers in Education" Department or bring multiple copies of the newspaper to the class session.
- Review adjectives and adverbs ("describing" words).
- Select one article for all of the students to read.
- As the students read that article, they are to underline all adverbs and adjectives in the piece.
- Have students work with partners to rewrite the article replacing all of the adjectives and adverbs with other describing words.
- Have student pairs read aloud their best (funniest, most absurd, most changed in meaning, etc) two or three altered sentences.
- Discuss why describing words are important in all types of writing.

<u>High School</u>

- Select some age-appropriate fictional pieces of writing that are considered to be good literature.
- Distribute copies of excerpts from these pieces to small groups of students.
- Have students discuss the word choices of the writer.
- Assign the students to rewrite the selection on a computer and, if available, determine the readability level of the piece by using the readability statistics function of the word processing software.
- Have students discuss the importance of the readability level in writing. Give an example of literature, such as *Alice in Wonderland*, that is difficult to read but appears to be written for a lower readability level.
- Discuss the importance of choosing words that are appropriate for each selected writing effort.

Images

Curriculum Tie-in: Art

<u>Elementary</u>

- Ask if any students have ever had a "bad" picture taken and allow them to share their stories.
- Have students decide on a famous person who is often in the news, such as the President of the United States.
- Have them bring photos of the selected person to the next class session.
- Have each student hold up one of these photos and have the class decide whether or not the photo is flattering.
- Explain to the students that someone "behind the scenes" made a choice to use this particular photo. Ask why anyone would choose an unflattering photo of this person to use in a newspaper or magazine.
- Discuss reasons why certain photos are selected.
- Have the class make a collage of the photos.
- Add to the collage as students bring in more photos of this person and discuss each photo.

<u>Middle School</u>

- Explain that the lesson is about images.
- Have small groups of students make lists of places where they see images.
- Compile the groups' ideas onto a list on butcher paper or a white board.
- Ask whether images in the media are always real. Have students explain how images can be altered.
- Discuss special effects and how some things that look real, like the dinosaurs in the movie, "Jurassic Park," are not necessarily real.
- Show a video about special effects, invite a professional from a media company, or have students use the Internet to learn more about special effects.
- Have the students write an essay about special effects.

<u>High School</u>

- Collect copies of tabloid newspapers or have students bring some to the next class session.
- In small groups have the students discuss both the images and stories on the front page of one of the tabloids.
- Introduce the concept of a "hierarchy of believability".
- Have students discuss whether what they see and read in tabloids is real.

- Have students select an actual photograph to use (scan a photograph or use the Internet to download a photo).
- Assignment: Use image manipulation software (for example, Adobe PhotoShop) to alter or distort the image.
- Have students share their new photographs.
- Discuss why photographs can no longer be considered "real" as evidence of truth.

Hierarchy of Believability

The desired result of training in critical thinking is an ability to discern the truth from among many information sources. It is desirable that one neither believes everything nor rejects everything—to be neither sponge nor cynic. Each adult person has, after years of testing different sources of information, built an informal, functioning hierarchy of believability regarding those innumerable sources. Some sources are found to be consistently dependable, have earned a high degree of respect, and the information is accepted with little hesitation. An example of a very high degree of believability is information presented in the *World Book Encyclopedia*. There the facts concerning, for instance, the death of Abraham Lincoln, are acknowledged as truthful and there is no felt need to further research the subject. Other sources such as local newspaper advertisements have earned less credibility. Still other sources like tabloid newspapers have little reliability among most adults. Without conscious effort, each person establishes, over time, his own hierarchy of believability among the many sources he encounters.

Students may not have a fully functioning hierarchy of believability, but most are somewhere in the process of creating one as they learn that not all sources are equal in worth. How does the media specialist or teacher encourage development of this hierarchy in students? The educator can: 1) offer opportunities to research various media and many sources of information; 2) encourage the students to think about various sources and to make decisions as to which ones are best for which types of information; and 3) provide several sources for students to use to find facts they need. Eventually the desired hierarchy will develop through discussion and research.

Fact vs. Opinion
Curriculum Tie-in: Language Arts and English
Elementary

- Have magazines available for students to use during this lesson.
- Ask students to attempt to define the words "fact" and "opinion." Then have one student find and share the definitions in a dictionary.
- Ask each student to state one fact.
- Ask each student to share an opinion.
- Discuss how they know the facts are true. Discuss how they know the opinions are true.
- Ask who among the students can explain the difference between a fact and an opinion.
- Distribute magazines to each pair of students.
- Have each pair of students find one fact and one opinion in the magazine and write them on paper.

- Allow time for students to share their findings. Let the class determine whether each stated example was indeed a fact or an opinion.
- Reinforce this concept often during the school year, asking whether a specific sentence that students are reading together is a fact or an opinion.

Middle School

- Have students define "fact" and "opinion."
- Discuss where in the media one would frequently find facts and where one would find opinions.
- Distribute copies from page 48 of Reproducible 3.3, "Fact or Opinion?"
- Assignment: Determine whether these typical statements found in media messages are facts or opinions.
- Students will share their answers and their reasoning.
- Have them discuss other media examples of facts and opinions that they have seen or heard.

High School

- Allow students to work with partners at computers.
- Ask them to visit the following Web site: <www.movies.com> and select a current movie that they have not seen.
- Students are to read the information and reviews about the movie, and compile five facts and three opinions.
- Allow time for students to share the facts and opinions about the selected movies.
- Assignment: Create a valid checklist to distinguish a fact from an opinion.
- Post the student-created checklists at the computers for other students to use.

Fiction or Nonfiction

Curriculum Tie-in: Information Literacy and Library Skills

Elementary

- Select 30 age-appropriate nonfiction books plus 30 age-appropriate fiction books to use with this lesson.
- Review the difference between fiction and nonfiction books.
- Read aloud an excerpt from a fiction book. Have students answer how they know it is fiction.
- Read aloud an excerpt from a nonfiction book. Have students answer how they know it is nonfiction.
- Give each student one fiction book and one nonfiction book.
- Assignment: Read at least three pages of each book. Copy one

statement or paragraph from each of the books. Use this excerpt to justify whether each book is fiction or nonfiction.
- Allow time for students to share their answers.
- Ask: Why does it make a difference whether you recognize the book or written work is fiction or nonfiction? How does this affect your thinking while reading the book?

Middle School

- Select a current movie that is based on a real person or event in history.
- Discuss the focus of the movie.
- Have the students decide whether this movie is real or made up.
- Assign students to research facts about this person or historical event and write down their findings.
- Allow the students to share the facts they found.
- Ask students to watch the movie and write a reaction paper about its factual accuracy.
- Discuss how media makers add details, characters, or dialogue to a movie to enhance it.
- Have the students revisit their decision about whether this movie is real or made up based on what they now know.

High School

- Assign each student to select a novel that was based on the life of a famous person.
- Assignment: Read that novel and list some specific facts about the famous person.
- Assign each student to locate and read a biography about that same person; confirm or refute the facts that were mentioned in the novel.
- Assignment: Write a comparison of the novel's information with the facts found in the biography. Were all of the facts accurate? Were there some discrepancies? Did the author of the novel take any liberties with the facts?
- Discuss why it is important to research the facts that are found in fiction writing or other fictional portrayals.

Summary
Curriculum Tie-in: Language Arts and English
Elementary

- Select an age-appropriate fiction book to read to the students, plus have on hand several others that contain summaries on their back covers.
- Review the meaning of the word "summarize."

- Share several examples of summaries that are found on the back covers of books. Explain that book summaries are used to let each reader know whether the book is the right one for him or her.
- Read a portion of a fiction book and then ask a student to summarize the events to that point. Remind students to include characters, setting, and important events in their summaries.
- Continue reading the story, stopping occasionally to have a student summarize each section.
- After reading the book, ask students to summarize the book in a concise and complete way, either orally or in writing.
- Use this activity often when reading aloud to students.

Middle School

- Review the meaning of the word "summarize."
- Remind students that story summaries include characters, setting, and important events.
- Discuss where summaries can be found in our culture.
- Assignment: Select and view a sitcom (situation comedy) that can be seen on television. Write a concise and complete summary of that program.
- Allow students to share their summaries with the class.
- Have students vote on the best summary.

High School

- Review the meaning of the word "summarize."
- Remind students that story summaries include characters, setting, and important events.
- Discuss some places where summaries can be found in our culture.
- Have students select an appropriate popular song or music video.
- Assignment: Write a concise and complete summary of that song or music video.
- Have students post their summaries on the school's Web site or in the school newspaper.

Sequence

Curriculum Tie-in: Language Arts and English
Elementary

- Collect the comic strip sections from the Sunday newspaper in preparation for this lesson.
- Discuss the word, "sequence."
- Review that stories have a beginning, middle, and an end, and often have many events that happen in the middle.
- Give each student one comic strip, a pair of scissors, and a business-

size envelope.
- Have the students carefully cut the comic strips into frames and put the frames into the envelopes.
- Collect and distribute the envelopes.
- Assignment: Students are to remove the comic strip frames from the envelopes, place them in the correct order, and then read their sequenced comic strips.
- Repeat this lesson as time allows.
- Discuss why sequence is important.

Middle School

- Obtain multiple copies of a local or regional newspaper.
- Review the word, "sequence."
- Discuss why it is necessary to understand the sequence of events or ideas.
- Give each student a copy of the sports section of the newspaper.
- Assignment: Select one sports story from the newspaper. Use a graphic organizer to show the following parts of the story: setting, characters, and events including the beginning, middle, and ending.
- Have students share or display their projects.

Curriculum Tie-in: History
High School:

- Have students each select a war from United States or world history.
- Have students research this war, using print, electronic, or Internet sources, collecting facts or events that happened before the war broke out, during the war, at the resolution of the war, and after the war.
- Assignment: Using the gathered facts, create a timeline illustrating the sequence of events that happened before, during, and after the war.
- Share these timelines with other classes in oral reports or displays in the hallways or other common areas in the school.

Statistics
Curriculum Tie-in: Math
Elementary

- Obtain multiple copies of a local newspaper and distribute one to each student.
- Assignment: Locate and cut out at least three graphs, tables, or charts from the newspaper and tape them to separate pages in your journals. Write one or two sentences below each graph, table, or chart in your journals, explaining the facts that are represented there.
- Have each student choose one of the graphs, tables, or charts in the

journal, explain the information to the rest of the class, and answer questions from other students about the information.

Middle School

- Have students save empty cereal boxes and bring them to the class for this lesson.
- Discuss the concept of good nutrition and the proper foods to eat to have a healthy body.
- Use a full box of cereal and measure out the amount that is considered a "serving," as identified in the nutrition information on the box. Discuss the amount of cereal in one "serving."
- Give each small group of students an empty cereal box.
- Have students read the nutritional information on the sides of the cereal boxes.
- Have students use the Internet to locate government information about the food triangle and the proper balance of food groups.
- Assignment: Compare the nutritional information on the cereal box to what is considered a healthy breakfast.
- Discussion: Why is nutritional information listed on cereal boxes? Is there anything misleading anywhere on the cereal box? What information is missing from the nutritional analysis?
- Discussion: Are statistics ever misleading?

High School

- Discuss how advertising can influence the public.
- Have students use the Internet to learn the statistics about the cost of advertising for the World Series baseball games, football's Super Bowl, or a current popular television program.
- Have students use the following Web site to find math-related articles and information: <http://medialit.med.sc.edu/ mathinthemedia.htm>
- Assignment: Based on the collected information about advertising costs, write and submit an essay about the power of advertising.
- Invite a professional from the advertising industry to come to the next class session to answer students' questions.

Name _____

Date _____

An **icon** is an easily-recognized symbol that represents a company, product, or other item.

A **slogan** is a short phrase that is used to identify a product or group.

A **jingle** is a catchy tune or verse that is usually used to sell a product or service.

Become aware of the icons, slogans, and jingles all around you.

List below at least five of each, along with the products they represent.

Icons:

Slogans:

Jingles:

Use the other side of this paper to create an icon, slogan, or jingle for your family to use.

Components of a Media Message

Each of these components is important to a media message:

- background or border

- props

- main focus

- people or animals

- colors (or black and white)

- photographs, drawings, or computer generated images

- purpose

- point of view

- text (words)

- visuals

- product or sponsor

- target audience

- tone (serious, humorous)

- hidden message

- personal reactions

Name _____

Date _____

Decide whether each of these statements is a fact or an opinion.

Mark each with an "F" or an "O."

Everyone enjoys going to the movies.

Crime is growing at an alarming rate in our city.

Our tortilla chips have no artificial ingredients.

The new shopping mall will be the best one yet.

Native Americans were the first to make popcorn.

Buy our candy bar and you'll enjoy every bite.

Clothes make the man.

You'll pay less interest on this ABC credit card.

This gift subscription will make your mom happy.

Our radio station plays more songs every hour.

Our cheesecake is light and fluffy.

These shoes will make you play like a pro.

50% off all lamps in our store through Saturday!

We have more items for you to choose from.

"Destiny Rides" will be shown at 6 and 8 pm today.

You'll love our prices!

We print the facts you need to know.

The forest fire in Nevada consumed 1000 acres.

John is the best player on the team.

There are only 46 shopping days until Christmas.

On the back of this page, explain why you think it's important to recognize the difference between facts and opinions.

CHAPTER FOUR

HOW WAS THE MESSAGE DELIVERED?

The list of our sources of information and entertainment in our culture is ever lengthening. The mass media make up a commanding portion of these sources. For a medium of communication to be considered a "mass medium," it must meet two criteria: it must use technology, and it must reach many people at once.

It is important to investigate the delivery formats used in the media messages encountered on a daily basis. Some of these delivery formats have become so effective in the communication of information and entertainment that our society, to varying degrees, has become dependent on them. In fact, many younger students cannot even imagine a world without televisions or computers. Recent statistics claim that students spend an average of three hours per day watching television, and some studies assert that teenagers now spend even more time on the Internet than they do viewing television. There is even discussion of these activities in terms of addictions. Just when it appeared that television watching was the primary competition for students' attention to school activities, the Internet has developed into an even more powerful attraction, at least to certain age and socioeconomic groups. The Internet as a communications format has revolutionized many aspects of our daily lives in a relatively short time.

"The Medium Is the Message."

Marshall McLuhan is credited with this remark. He was a Canadian scholar, a professor, an author, a lecturer, and certainly a visionary. Even today, when people hear his often-quoted statement, "the medium is the message" there are looks of puzzlement. However, he well understood the mass media and their impact.

McLuhan's idea can best be grasped by considering the following two scenarios:

Scenario #1:

You are with students in the classroom or the library media center. Suddenly over the public address system you hear the voice of the principal. The principal asks for everyone's attention and shares some important information. What is actually happening during this announcement? You might be finishing your preparation for the next lesson or checking attendance. Your students are in all likelihood whispering, reading, or finishing homework assignments. In essence, even though there is a message being delivered, few are focused and attentive.

Scenario #2:

The principal comes to your classroom or library and asks to speak with the students. She delivers the exact same words in the identical manner as in scenario #1, only this time in person in the room face-to-face with the students. Notice your body language. You are listening and looking at the principal and so are the students. There might be one or two who are busy with other things, but most are giving the principal their rapt attention.

What was the difference? Clearly the message was the same in both situations. The same principal shared the same words in both scenarios. The only difference was the method in which the message was delivered. The message was not the main point; it was the system utilized to deliver the message. In the first instance, the delivery was via an impersonal and electronic mass medium. In the second, a human being was talking directly to you and the students. Evidently, as McLuhan wrote, "the medium is the message." Students must be taught to pay attention to how the message is delivered because it has everything to do with the reaction and impact of that message.

Using Video

Teacher use of videotapes and DVDs in the classroom is rampant. Certainly expanded knowledge and experiences can be imparted through these formats, but videos must be utilized with discretion and with purpose.

Context and Visual Clues

Understanding the context of a media message is fundamental to its comprehension. The conveyed information may be true only within the specific context of the message and cannot, therefore, be generalized to other situations. A single sentence in a news article, for example, might not represent the article's actual content. Receiving information out of context has always been an issue. In this world of soundbites and 15-second television news stories, it is imperative that investigation of the context and the exact meaning of the media message be addressed. Critical thinking is the goal, and students must develop the skill of looking beyond headlines and soundbites, researching the facts for themselves.

Figure 4.1: Viewing a Video

Viewing a Video

When considering the use of a videotape or DVD as part of a lesson plan, here are some tips to consider:

- The video should **always** be previewed before using it with students.
- A video does not have to be used in its entirety. Select the portion that best conveys the concept to be taught.
- Before showing the video, point out ideas or questions for the students to focus on. The class can be divided into small groups, with each group having a separate focus or question to answer. After viewing the video, students can share their comments and observations with the rest of the class.
- Avoid using a video as a reward.
- Pause frequently for discussion or to emphasize a concept.
- Rewind the tape and replay segments to reinforce concepts.
- Leave the lights on. The students will request that the lights be turned off, but the classroom is not a movie theater. Leaving the lights on allows the instructor to oversee the students, enables students to take notes, and permits the teacher or media specialist to more easily pause or rewind the video and lead discussions. Furthermore leaving the lights on reminds students that the expectation is that they be active participants, not passive spectators.
- Turn the television around or drape a towel over the screen to help students concentrate on the sounds, voices, and sound effects.
- Turn off the sound so students can concentrate on the images, characters, setting, props, background, and special effects.
- Use a video to introduce a concept, to expand student knowledge, to visit new places, or as a culminating experience.

The visual clues within the message provide extra information and, therefore, must be studied. Images and visuals inundate the majority of entertainment and news media formats. The axiom, "A picture is worth 1000 words," holds more true today than ever before. Visual clues offer information frequently not found in the text, can expand the overall understanding, and extend the memory for a longer period of time. Photojournalism is the discipline that shares emotional or sensational stories through photographs, and today's photographers compete for prizes. It is important not to be persuaded by photographs, however, since it is known that they can be altered.

The activities in this chapter provide lessons in which students learn to go beyond first impressions and gather details and facts before drawing conclusions.

Genre

Genre is a term customarily used for categories of artistic or literature styles, but it can be generalized to other media. We teach the genre of literature, such as mysteries, poetry, and historical fiction, but that is just a starting place, since this term can be broadened to include other media. One of the activities in this chapter uses the arrangement of the local movie rental store as a starting point and considers it as a system for organizing books based on category for their home or classroom. By relating a known entity in our culture to this educational term, students come away with a deeper understanding and lasting memory of the word "genre."

Capturing the Audience

One of the foundational principles of the mass media is that they must capture the attention of the viewer, reader, or listener. Whether the message is in a picture book or on a poster, a T-shirt, a For Sale sign, or the front page of a newspaper, the first step is to capture the attention of the audience. Teaching students this principle will help students internalize skills that will be needed on achievement tests.

Students will recognize techniques in print media that are used to capture the attention of the reader. Then, as they write, they can incorporate these methods into their own writing. Some of the ways students can improve their writing to capture the attention of the reader are through the use of dialogue, questions, humor, quotations, uncommon expressions, or unusual format.

Poetry

The mere mention of the word poetry as a topic for study can lose most students' interest. Poetry has been beaten to death in the typical classroom, partially because it does not, on the surface, appear to be relevant to today's children and teenagers. The trick is to find a foothold and make poetry come alive as an art form and literature genre. As students discover that most of today's music is actually poetry put to music, they might sing a different tune about the study of poetry.

Poetry is emotional, sincere, or intense writing in a verse format. Students need to know how to recognize, interpret, and write poetry. Music holds the key! Songs are, for the most part, poems put to music. The activities in this chapter can be coordinated with the music teacher and a new professional partnership can emerge. In addition, students may appreciate the music teacher in a new way when they learn the relationship between songs and poetry. The immediate result might be that students become poets, even though they might prefer the label "lyricists."

Media literacy bridges the gap between the culture surrounding the students and their world of school. Widening the students' general understanding of the world around them will make these skills a permanent part of their thinking.

ACTIVITIES

"The Medium is the Message."
Curriculum Tie-in: Art
<u>Elementary</u>

- Review the words "media" and "format."
- Have students work in small groups, each making a list of the various media that are in our culture. Compile the lists onto butcher paper for future reference.
- Ask students to brainstorm ideas for a message that the students in their school need to be reminded of (for example, there should be no graffiti in the school). The students should select the best message to use in this lesson.
- Have the small groups each adopt that same message but use a different medium to distribute it (for example, one group creates a Web site, another a poster, another a bumper sticker).
- After the students complete their messages, have them share their results with the class, and compare and contrast the potential impact of the various media.
- Discussion: Since the message was exactly the same, why did it matter which medium was used to deliver it? Which medium was the best for this message and would most likely be able to reach the target audience—the students at their school?
- Have students choose the best medium to get the message across to the students at their school. If practical, display the resulting media product on a bulletin board or in another prominent place.

<u>Middle School</u>

- Assign students to do research to learn about Marshall McLuhan and share the findings with the class.
- Share his statement, "The medium is the message." Lead students in a discussion of what McLuhan might have meant by this.
- Assignment: Work in small groups. Take McLuhan's statement and create a mural that interprets its meaning for others.
- Have students explain their murals and then display them in the hallways.
- Discussion: What are the ramifications of this statement?

<u>High School</u>

- Share the statement, "The medium is the message." Lead students in a discussion of what McLuhan might have meant by this.

- Discussion: In art, various media are used. List some of the different media that artists use, and discuss why and when one medium might be a better choice than another.
- Assignment: Choose one famous artist, such as Rembrandt, Grandma Moses, or Norman Rockwell. Research that artist's life and work. Write an essay defending the art medium the artist chose to use.
- Assign students to make oral presentations to the class about their selected artists and display representative work of the artists.
- After each presentation, have the class discuss the artist and the medium used.
- Discuss how the statement, "The medium is the message," relates to art.

Context and Visual Clues

Curriculum Tie-in: Language Arts and English

<u>Elementary</u>

- Subscribe to an age-appropriate news magazine to be delivered to the class.
- Select one sentence from a news article and read it aloud. Ask the students to guess what the article covers.
- Have students read the news article together and discuss it.
- Check to see how many of them had the right idea about the content of the article. Explain that taking a sentence out of context is unfair in that it might not adequately represent the article.
- Repeat this activity often during the school year, each time explaining that one has to read the entire article to know precisely what the author is saying.

<u>Middle School</u>

- Discuss visuals and their importance.
- Discussion: Why is television news so popular? What is the main difference between television news and radio news? What can you gain by watching (as opposed to merely hearing) the news?
- Videotape a local or regional television newscast.
- Discuss the importance of television news.
- Have students watch a portion of the television newscast without the sound. Discuss reactions.
- Have students listen to another portion of the newscast without the picture (turn the television around or drape a towel over the screen). Discuss reactions.
- Have students listen to another portion of the newscast without the picture and write down facts about the news story. Compile a list of these facts.

- Rewind the tape and have students watch the same portion of the newscast with the picture noting any facts they missed while listening the first time.
- Add all of the new facts to the list.
- Discussion: Why do visuals give you a better understanding of the news story? Which medium of news do you prefer?
- Assignment: Write a letter to the news station with reactions and comments about the importance of visuals in news reports.

High School

- Locate a Web site that is a good source for the written scripts of the U.S. President's speeches.
- Print copies of the entire script of a recent speech by the president.
- Discuss the word "soundbite."
- Explain that due to time or space constraints the news industry often selects a portion of a speech to include in the print or broadcast news.
- Give each student a copy of the president's speech.
- Assignment: Read the president's speech. Select and write down a soundbite that best summarizes the content of the president's speech.
- Have each student read aloud the soundbite that was selected.
- Discussion: Why didn't each student select the same section? Why is it necessary to read an entire speech for yourself? What happens when a reporter or editor takes a sentence or section out of the context of the speech? What are the ramifications?
- Invite a reporter to the next class session to discuss how soundbites are chosen for news reports. Allow students to ask questions about the selection process.

Genre

Curriculum Tie-in: Language Arts and Information Literacy
Elementary

- Have students decide on their favorite television programs.
- Have each student take a turn adding his favorite television program to a butcher paper display.
- Read the list aloud.
- Ask students to think of categories that these programs would fit into (for example, sports, cartoons, sitcoms) and group the listed programs into these categories.
- Have the students name other categories of television programs that are not on their list.
- Introduce the term "genre" and explain that genre means category or art form.
- Explain that literature can be divided into several genre. Ask students to come up with categories for books in the library. Compile a list of their ideas.

- Place their list on the wall with the word "genre" on it and add other categories as students think of them. Refer to this list every time the word "genre" is mentioned during the school year.

<u>Middle School</u>

- Ask who has ever been to a movie rental store.
- Ask students to name the sections, such as "action," "family," and "cartoon," that are used in movie rental stores. Compile a list of the categories.
- Explain that the library's classification system arranges books in an organized way. Books in a home or classroom could be shelved by categories like the movies at video rental stores.
- Ask students to suggest categories for the books. Compile a list of their ideas. Review the list and edit it as needed.
- Explain that the suggestions on the list are called "genre," and that "genre" is another name for categories.
- Have each small group of students select a literature genre and create a poster to describe it.
- Display their posters in the library in the appropriate locations to help students find the various categories of books.

Curriculum Tie-in: Music
<u>High School</u>

- Have students list names for the different styles of music they know.
- Make a compiled list adding to it as other styles are mentioned.
- Review and discuss the word "genre."
- Assignment: Research one genre of music from the list and write a report about it. Locate a sample of this genre of music on record, audiotape, or CD and bring it to class.
- Have students share their reports and their sample of the music with the rest of the class, followed by discussion of this style of music.
- Use the term "genre" when discussing categories of music and other arts.

Poetry

Curriculum Tie-in: Music
<u>Elementary</u>

- Discuss poetry as a style of writing.
- Read aloud poems on a regular basis and have students discuss each one including the author's choice of poetry as a style of writing, the author's purpose, and their personal reactions.
- Explain that the lyrics of most songs are actually poems.
- Distribute copies of Reproducible 4.1 located on page 58 to every student and have them read the lyrics of "The Star-Spangled Banner."

- Review words in the lyrics that are new to the students.
- Read aloud the story of the writing of this song. Use an encyclopedia, a history book, or the Internet to locate a brief background about the song.
- Discuss reasons why the author might have chosen to write this story as a song or poem.
- Have each student rewrite each stanza in his own words.
- Have the students listen to the music of "The Star-Spangled Banner" without singing the words.
- Then have the students sing the song together.
- Assignment: Write your reaction to the lyrics of the song, and explain why it is considered our national anthem.
- Discussion: What is the difference between a poem and a story? Why are the lyrics of most songs actually poetry?

Middle School

- Discuss poetry as a style of writing.
- Explain that the lyrics of most songs are actually poems.
- Assignment: Select one popular song that has acceptable lyrics and bring a copy of the lyrics to the next class session. Write a summary of the song and list your thoughts about why the song was written.
- Have each student share the song's lyrics and have the class decide whether the lyrics of each song are actually poetry.
- Discussion: What is a poem? What is the difference between a poem and a story? Why are the lyrics of most songs actually poetry?

High School

- Discussion: What is a poem? What is the difference between a poem and a story? Why are the lyrics of most songs actually poetry?
- Direct students to brainstorm about popular songs and select an appropriate one to discuss. Have one student agree to locate the lyrics of that song and bring them to the next class session.
- Make a transparency of the lyrics of the selected song, and show the transparency to the class.
- Ask the students to read these lyrics and discuss whether the lyrics are actually a poem.
- Assignment: Rewrite the lyrics in your own words. Explain possible reasons why this song was written.
- Discussion: Why do some songs become popular and others seem to disappear quickly from the play lists at the radio stations or from the music videos on television?
- Assignment: Write a poem about something important to you. Add music to the words and create a song, using the poem as the lyrics.
- Have students share their songs with the class.

"The Star-Spangled Banner"

Francis Scott Key, 1814

O say, can you see, by the dawn's early light,
What so proudly we hail'd at the twilight's last gleaming?
Whose broad stripes and bright stars, thro' the perilous fight,
O'er the ramparts we watch'd, were so gallantly streaming?
And the rockets' red glare, the bombs bursting in air,
Gave proof thro' the night that our flag was still there.
O say, does that star-spangled banner yet wave
O'er the land of the free and the home of the brave?

On the shore dimly seen thro' the mists of the deep,
Where the foe's haughty host in dread silence reposes,
What is that which the breeze, o'er the towering steep,
As it fitfully blows, half conceals, half discloses?
Now it catches the gleam of the morning's first beam,
In full glory reflected, now shines on the stream:
'Tis the star-spangled banner: O, long may it wave
O'er the land of the free and the home of the brave!

And where is that band who so vauntingly swore
That the havoc of war and the battle's confusion,
A home and a country should leave us no more?
Their blood has wash'd out their foul footsteps' pollution.
No refuge could save the hireling and slave
From the terror of flight or the gloom of the grave:
And the star-spangled banner in triumph doth wave
O'er the land of the free and the home of the brave.

O thus be it ever when free-men shall stand
Between their lov'd home and the war's desolation;
Blest with vict'ry and peace, may the heav'n-rescued land
Praise the Pow'r that hath made and preserv'd us a nation!
Then conquer we must, when our cause it is just,
And this be our motto: "In God is our trust!"
And the star-spangled banner in triumph shall wave
O'er the land of the free and the home of the brave!

CHAPTER FIVE

WHAT IS THE IMPACT OF THE MESSAGE ON ME?

Living in a culture under a ceaseless bombardment of literally thousands of media messages presents a struggle to constantly sort and evaluate their worth. Not all messages are equal in their merit to us as individuals. Some are worthy of analysis and some are not. There is no way to spend the time necessary to evaluate every media message. The result is that individuals might all too haphazardly view, hear, or read messages without adequate criteria for selection and retention. Part of the process of becoming critical thinkers is to decide which messages are necessary to remember due to their real value and which ones can be dismissed.

Once certain messages are selected—those that seem to have content of value—they must be assessed regarding their personal impact and significance. The trick is to make the effort to comprehend and analyze, and then to react to those messages.

Many of the activities in this chapter require that students keep journals as a vehicle for their personal responses. Instructors who are experienced in use of the journal strategy have come to realize the significance of some specific policies. For instance, it is critical not to grade the journal entries. It is important to regularly read the entries and write personal comments, but as soon as a teacher values one student's journal contents worthy of an "A," all the students quickly discern that it is not about writing honest and personal responses, but about "playing the game" and answering in a way that triggers good grades. Furthermore, to ensure that journal writing remains an opportunity for students to respond without peer pressure and without concerns that their classmates may read or hear their thoughts, the journals should never be read aloud, even anonymously. It is better to ask if anyone would like to share her journal entry, which puts the student in charge of whether or not to disclose what was written. Journal entries might provide the only time students can respond with true feelings, without worrying about being socially or politically correct. It is, of course, necessary for students to complete their journal entries because journals are not optional assignments. Keep in mind that all writers are hungry for feedback regarding their work. This is not a time to correct grammar but an opportunity to connect at a deeper level. The purpose of journal writing is to allow the free flow of personal reactions. Providing students this chance to write in journals may facilitate the building of rapport between students and teachers or media specialists, and thereby sanction honesty at a deeper level. In addition, it might cause students to discover that writing can be a catharsis—an experience that brings to the surface sincere emotions that have been heretofore untapped.

Writing exercises make students aware of their power to express themselves. This human need for personal expression can be a vehicle to prepare students for state assessments, where they will need to write. Even more important, these experiences might introduce students to a type of writing that can last a lifetime. Journaling is popular and is therapeutic for many people.

What is the impact of the message on me? This is a profound and complicated question. Not every message must have an impact. In fact, most messages are flushed away almost as quickly as they are seen, heard, or read. There are some that stay with us, that are important enough for us to think about and evaluate, and others that can actually have life-changing implications.

The skills students need for those state assessment tests are the same skills that are necessary to become thoughtful, conscientious citizens in a democracy. Consider this quote by an anonymous thinker:

> "A good education can't make leaders out of all of us … but it can teach us which leaders to follow."

Not every student will have the opportunity to become President of the United States, but every one of them can vote for a President … and for many other candidates and issues during his lifetime.

Our democracy requires that voters be involved and discerning critical thinkers. As students begin to think about media messages—including political ones—they are preparing for their role as citizens in our democracy.

Students will make decisions every day regarding their health, lifestyles, appearance, language, clothing, friends, leisure time activities, entertainment choices, educational options, future careers, and hundreds of other significant matters. For them to consider the consequences of their decisions is vital for safe and healthy lives. However, there is no identifiable unit of instruction that consistently develops skills in decision-making and evaluation. The teaching of media literacy—critical thinking about media messages—is essential and timely, and must be merged into all extant curricula if it is to rise to the surface in any classroom. The media specialist or classroom teacher has the opportunity to impact lives in a new and dynamic way. The educator who looks beyond the standard curriculum and helps each student make a personal connection with the culture around him is performing a significant role. Only when critical thinking training is fully merged into existing lessons can students become capable of making decisions that will positively impact their lives.

The skills offered in this chapter can open doors to critical thinking, not in a traditional or mundane way, but with a fresh and relevant approach. At the same time, these are the skills required for success on any state assessment.

Content and Format Revisited

In Chapter 3, "What Is the Message?" students studied various aspects of the content of messages and they were then introduced to the process of analysis. Then in Chapter 4, "How Was the Message Delivered?" they focused on the format of messages. In this chapter, they will again look at these elements, but now the purpose is more individualized. The content and format will trigger personal responses. Now is the time to encourage the "3 Rs" of media literacy: review, reflect, and react.

Extraction of Meaningful Information

The next step is to isolate any significant information in the message. Is there any meat to this message or can it be tossed out? How does one capture and summarize the essence of the message? The activities in this portion of the chapter will allow students to practice this skill. It must become second nature to students so that it happens immediately. The purpose of using media messages to prepare students for assessment tests is to practice these skills so they will transfer to real-life situations. Isolated learning in schools often has little bearing on the rest of the students' lives, but the use of media messages makes learning authentic by guaranteeing there will be enhanced transfer of learning to life.

Interpretation

Interpretations of a media message will vary from person to person depending on each one's individual characteristics. To interpret the message, a person must be able to relate to it. If the message is so foreign to one's thinking, there might be no reaction at all other than curiosity. Consider a McDonald's Restaurant advertisement that is written in the Russian language. Although there is familiarity with some of the imagery—perhaps the golden arches—there cannot be complete interpretation of this message due to a lack of comprehension. To interpret a media message, there are important questions for students to ask:

- "What is the message?"
- "How will I interpret this message?"
- "Is this significant to my thinking or my life?"

The more students question, the more they think. This is the goal.

Figure 5.1: The "3 Rs" of Media Literacy

The "3 Rs" of Media Literacy
Review   Reflect   React

To **review** is to contemplate the various aspects of the message: the words, text, or script; the colors; the characters; the background or setting; the music or voice; and the overall idea or theme.

After watching a sitcom on television, the viewer might consider the story line, the characters, the dialogue, the climax, and the humor. She thinks about the actors who played the various parts, their clothing and hairstyles, the music, and the setting for the program.

To **reflect** is to consider the implications of the message. Questions might be: What are the opinions, attitudes, beliefs, values, and norms that are blatantly or subtly shared in this message? Who created this message and why? How do I feel about this message? Do I agree or disagree with the stated premise? How does this message make me feel?

The person who watched the sitcom now thinks about the attitudes of the characters, the opinions expressed in the show, values that were apparent, and the impact of the program. She compares what was shared with her own personal beliefs and ideas. She makes decisions about whether she agrees with such aspects as the premise of the show, the humor, and the conclusions.

To **react** implies there is some action needed. This response might be an overt action or a change in personal thinking. The reaction could also be a confirmation of one's previously held ideas.

Now the viewer of the sitcom can take action. Perhaps she enjoyed the program and decides to watch it again next week. She might have liked it well enough to tell her friends about the program and encourage them to watch. On the other hand she might have been offended, and decides to never watch the sitcom again. If she is very upset, she might call the local television station that aired the program or even write a letter to the producer or sponsors of the show.

These "3 Rs" can be the standard formula for this part of the media literacy experience. The main objective of media literacy is to cause people to be critical thinkers and have reactions to the media's messages, not merely to allow the messages to influence lives without contemplation. Reviewing the content and format of those messages that are considered worthwhile is essential, but that is only the first step. It is also important to take time to reflect and react to the messages.

Comparisons

In the *GrassRoots Taxonomy of Thinking Skills* (see Figure 1.3, Chapter 1), the levels of critical thinking are offered. "Compare and contrast" is listed as a higher-level thinking strategy. Comparing and contrasting different media messages and how they impact the audience is an ongoing media literacy skill. The activities offered here will jumpstart the thinking among students and will excite them about their own judgments. The very idea that in this case there are no real "right or wrong" answers is empowering to young people. Here, at last, is an opportunity to express an opinion without fear of rejection or failure. Individual thinking is rewarded, and the higher the level of thinking, the better.

Reliability

Assessing the reliability of a message might be the most fundamental of the media literacy skills. It is essential that each individual be able to determine the reliability of the source of the information. The Internet has upset our "hierarchy of believability" (see Figure 3.2 on page 40). In the past, it was easier to determine the source of information and make decisions about whether to believe the source. It was never foolproof, but there was at least some system to follow. Now the world is available "24/7" via the Internet, and there is no longer the guarantee of gatekeepers to filter the information. The Internet is the world, with all of its infinite ramifications. Determining reliability is a complex skill involving extensive examination of the source and certainly cannot be taught in one or two lessons. Each of us is continuously updating our personal hierarchy of believability based on events in our daily lives. To question the reliability of the source is, indeed, the first step in the believability process.

How Do We Determine the Reliability of a Web Site?

The Internet has revolutionized research and many aspects of our daily lives, but how can we determine whether the information on a Web site is dependable?

Kathy Schrock is a leading authority in this field and has developed an important resource for teachers. She states:

"Unlike the media center, there are no media specialists to sort out the valuable information from the substandard information. With more than 350 million documents available on the Web alone, finding relevant information online can be daunting. Therefore, the ability to critically evaluate information is an invaluable skill in this information age. The acquisition of digital literacy skills is dependent upon the student's ability to find information, determine its usefulness, and utilize it effectively."

Schrock offers 26 criteria for determining the worth of information found on a Web site, such as evaluating whether the information contained on the Web site is biased, pertinent, verifiable, or dated. Kathy Schrock's material is offered for teacher use at <www.discoveryschool.com/schrockguide/eval.html>

In addition, there is a valuable Web site evaluation activity for middle school students called "Jo Cool or Jo Fool?" at <www.media-awareness.ca/english/special_initiatives/games/joecool_joefool/jo_ cool_teachers.cfm>

Main Idea and Supporting Details

Most writers write in a formula-driven manner, following precise rules and conventions. To extract the main idea and the supporting details from this piece of writing is not difficult. However what if it is not written material that is being analyzed? What impact does a message have if those conventions are not followed? There are times when extraction is more nebulous and painstaking. The activities in this chapter elicit recognition of the main idea and supporting details in various media messages.

Personal Reactions

Now is an ideal time to introduce the concept of individual differences followed by a discussion regarding possible reasons for the uniqueness of each person. One of the elementary activities in this chapter centers around individual uniqueness. Let the students brainstorm about differences that might cause people to react and interpret media messages in different ways. For example, students might mention family, lifestyle, gender, heritage, personal experiences, leisure time preferences, media involvement, values, travel, and still other differences. Emphasize that each person has personal opinions and thus is likely to have personal reactions to media messages. Consider this example: two teachers go to the movies together and view the same movie in the same theater. All the external elements are the same—the sound, the setting, the smells, the audience, the temperature, and the cost. However, as the teachers leave the theater and compare their impressions, it may well be that they come away with very different reactions—one liking the movie and being moved by the experience, the other disliking it and finding it depressing or lackluster. How could this happen when they experienced the same film? The answer lies within the composite of ingredients that make up each individual's personality. This concept might spearhead a discussion that students need to accept and appreciate each others' ideas and opinions and individual differences in general.

Personal Responsibilities

Living in a democracy necessitates that citizens be involved in the political process. It is not enough to be a thinker—involved in the analysis, interpretation, and evaluation of media messages. It is imperative that each citizen reflects on and reacts to messages and takes a stand, if necessary. This chapter's activities will focus on the discussion of responses and responsibilities. Later, in Chapter 7, "Make a Message," students will have the chance to create media messages and become actively involved in the responsibilities that come with freedom.

ACTIVITIES

Content and Format Revisited

Curriculum Tie-in: Art

<u>Elementary</u>

- Review the terms "content" and "format."
- Show some samples of artwork in various media or formats, such as paintings, graphics, ads, or sculpture.
- Ask the class to select one of the art pieces for further examination.
- Have students get their art journals and write the title of this piece of art on a new page.
- Assignment: Answer the following questions in your art journal:
    - "What do you like or dislike about this piece of art?"
    - "Why do you think the artist selected this medium (format) for his work?"
    - "What is the meaning or theme of this piece of art?"
    - "Could the artist have created the same meaning in another format?"
    - "Do you think this piece of art should be placed in an art museum?"
- Collect the journals, read their journal entries, respond to their answers, and return the journals to the students during the next class session.
- After returning the journals, once again read the questions aloud. Ask what the odds are that all student responses to these questions would be the same. Discuss why personal reaction and interpretation are part of art. Discuss what would happen if all artists had to use the same medium or format.
- Have students take turns orally sharing what medium (format) they would select if they were artists.

<u>Middle School</u>

- Use a transparency of Reproducible 5.1 on page 73 to introduce the "3 Rs of Media Literacy."
- Select a poster to use with this activity.
- Show the students the poster. Explain the three steps of analyzing the poster using this "3 Rs" approach.
- Show students the poster and ask them to use the review, reflect, and react process to analyze it.
- Give students copies of Reproducible 5.1.
- Assignment: Select five different media messages and complete the worksheet following the "3 Rs" process.
- During the next class session, allow students to share one of their

responses from the assignment. Discuss their reactions to this "3 Rs" approach.

- Use the "3 Rs" process often during the school year to reinforce this process.

<u>High School</u>

- Collect yearbooks from various schools or allow students to bring in their parents' yearbooks from home.
- Ask small groups of students to look through the yearbooks and discuss their formats.
- Discussion: How is their own school's yearbook different than the other yearbooks? How is it the same? What is the same in all of the school yearbooks? Why are the formats always similar?
- Have each group come up with a new format for school yearbooks and share it with the class. Discuss each format and decide if it is better than the one their school uses. Discuss why there will probably not be total agreement.

Extraction of Meaningful Information

Curriculum Tie-in: Social Studies
<u>Elementary</u>

- Subscribe to an age-appropriate news magazine for the class, such as *Time for Kids*.
- Distribute a current issue of the magazine to the students.
- Read aloud one article together.
- Ask students to suggest what information is the most meaningful from the article; write their ideas on a white board or butcher paper.
- Have them reread the listed ideas and suggest more concise ways of writing the article's most important information. Direct them to keep working on this task until there are succinct sentences stating just the most meaningful information.
- Explain that although we all have individual thoughts about what we read, hear, or see, it is possible to agree on the "meat" or essence from media messages.
- Repeat this lesson frequently during the school year.

<u>Middle School</u>

- Videotape the first few minutes of a local, regional, or national television news program.
- Show the first two minutes of the news program to the class.
- Have the students write down each news item and then the most important information from each news story. Explain that this is not a summary of what happened, but the fact or facts that were the most significant.

- Show the same two minutes of the video several times so students can complete this assignment.
- Ask students to share their responses for each news story. Discuss the most meaningful information for each news story.
- Repeat this activity several times during the school year so students can practice extracting meaningful information.

<u>High School</u>

- Collect a variety of current news magazines, such as *Time* or *Newsweek*.
- Discuss news magazines and how they are different from newspapers.
- Assignment: Select one article from a news magazine; make a copy of it; read it; list the most meaningful information from the article on a piece of paper; turn this paper in with the copy of the news story. Reminder: this is not a summary of the article, but a list of the most meaningful facts.
- Read the assignments and share your reactions.
- Repeat this lesson occasionally during the school year to reinforce the extraction of meaningful information.

Interpretation

Curriculum Tie-in: Music
<u>Elementary</u>

- Select a piece of music that the students have not heard in class.
- Discuss the word "interpretation" with students.
- Have students brainstorm about why people would interpret music in different ways and compile a list of their ideas on a white board or butcher paper.
- Hand out pencils, paper, crayons, and colored pencils.
- Assignment: While you listen to this music, create a picture of what you think this musical piece is about.
- Play the music.
- Direct students to share and explain their pictures after the music is over.
- Discuss why each person had a different interpretation.
- Repeat this activity often.

Curriculum Tie-in: Language Arts and English
<u>Middle School</u>

- Make Reproducible 5.2, "Reading Quotations," on page 74 into a transparency.
- Discuss the meaning of the word "interpret."
- Ask why people can have different interpretations of the same media messages.

- Discussion: Are books still important and relevant in this millennium? Is reading still a required skill?
- Show one of the quotes on the transparency (by covering the other quotes).
- Ask students to write down what they think the quote means.
- Have them share and discuss their responses. Ask again why people might interpret this quote in different ways.
- Repeat this activity using the other quotes from Reproducible 5.2 during other class sessions.

Curriculum Tie-in: Art
High School

- Select a piece of art that is unusual or not likely to have been seen before by students.
- Discuss the meaning of the word "interpret."
- Ask why people might have different interpretations of art.
- Have students write down what they think this piece of art conveys. Discuss their responses. Ask why people might interpret this art piece in different ways.
- Repeat this activity during other class sessions using new pieces of art.

Comparisons
Curriculum Tie-in: Information Literacy
Elementary

- Introduce the words "biography" and "autobiography."
- Assignment: Locate two biographies or autobiographies about the same person, either at the school or public library. Read both of the books and compare the information in them. Select a few facts or events that were different or omitted in one of the books and create a visual to share this information with the class.
- Display and discuss the students' work.
- Discussion: How could biographies about the same person have different information? Why is this important?

Middle School

- Assignment: Select a book to read that has been made into a movie or television program. Read the book; then watch the movie or program. Compare the two versions of the story on a two-sided chart. Write a paragraph about your impressions and which version you preferred.
- Ask students to share their findings.
- Discussion: Why are visual portrayals always different from the books on which they are based?

- Assignment: Select, read, and make a copy of a news story from a local, regional, or national newspaper. Locate a news story in another newspaper or news magazine about the same news item. Compare the two versions of the story, explain how this news story affects you, and turn this assignment in to the teacher or media specialist.
- Discussion: How can news stories in different media be different, and leave different impressions, when the facts are the same?
- Invite a reporter to the class to discuss different news sources, explain the news gathering process, and answer students' questions.

Reliability

Curriculum Tie-in: Information Literacy

Elementary

- Discuss the words "reliable" and "unreliable." Have students give examples of how these words can be used.
- Assignment: Write a journal entry explaining where your most reliable information comes from.
- Read their journal entries and respond to each one.
- Every time a new source of information is mentioned during the school year, ask whether it is a reliable source.

Middle School

- Explain that critical thinkers must be able to determine which sources are reliable.
- Have small groups of students generate lists of reliable and unreliable sources.
- Students then share their lists; discuss them; compile their ideas into two class lists: reliable sources and unreliable sources.
- Display the lists in the library or computer lab to help other students understand which sources of information are reliable.

High School

- Discuss the word "reliable."
- Students work in small groups to produce short skits to explain what the word "reliable" means.
- Have each group perform their skit for the rest of the class.
- Discuss why it is important to determine whether media messages are reliable.
- Have students perform their skits at an assembly or in an elementary or middle school classroom.

Main Idea and Supporting Details
Curriculum Tie-in: Social Studies
Elementary

- Select a video that is related to a topic being studied.
- Show one short segment of the video to the class.
- Ask students to write down the main idea and supporting details in this segment.
- Students then share their ideas and decide on the best answers.
- Repeat this activity during the remaining segments of this video to practice deciphering the main idea and the supporting details.

Middle School

- Locate an age-appropriate brief documentary film (current or historical). Use the Cable in the Classroom listings online <www.ciconline.com> or read the monthly *Access Learning* magazine to learn about documentaries offered via television.
- Show the first five minutes of this documentary. Have students determine the main idea and supporting details for this segment.
- Repeat this activity during the remaining segments of this video to practice deciphering the main idea and the supporting details.
- Direct students to write journal entries about their reactions to the documentary.
- Read and respond to their entries.

High School

- Select four or five age-appropriate essays and make copies of them.
- Discuss the difference between an essay and other styles of writing.
- Tell the class about the topics of the essays.
- Assignment: Select one essay; read it; write down the main idea and the supporting details.
- Ask all the students who selected the same essay to get together in a group and discuss their answers.
- Have each group decide on one main idea and a list of supporting details for their essay.
- Discussion: What is the difference between a theme in a fiction story and the main idea in an essay?
- Assignment: Select a topic; research it; write an essay; underline the main idea, and circle the supporting details.

Personal Reactions
Curriculum Tie-in: Language Arts and English
Elementary

- Collect 40-50 interesting newspaper photographs and tape them on sheets of construction paper.
- Discuss individual differences and the uniqueness of each individual. Emphasize that each one of us can have our own personal reactions to media messages.
- Introduce the term, "photojournalism." Assign students to use the dictionary to learn more about this word.
- Give each student a newspaper photo. Allow the class a few minutes to deconstruct their photos.
- Have students write personal reactions to the photos in their journals.
- Read their journal entries and write a response to every entry.

Middle School

- Have students bring magazine ads to class.
- Discuss peer pressure. Have students give examples of peer pressure in the media.
- Divide students into small groups and give magazine ads to each group.
- Assignment: Locate and discuss ads that represent examples of peer pressure. Select one to share with the class.
- Each group then shares with the class the ad that best exemplifies peer pressure.
- Assignment: Write a journal entry about how advertising influences you. Add ideas about how to keep this from happening in the future.
- Have students create posters using the ads to offset the pressure to conform. (For example, "Don't believe it—not EVERYONE is buying this!")
- Display the ads in the hallway or cafeteria.

High School

- Discuss individual differences and the uniqueness of each individual. Emphasize that each person can have his own personal reactions to media messages.
- Discuss editorial cartoons and show examples. (Use the Web sites listed in the Appendix, "Media Literacy Resources and Organizations" to locate editorial cartoons.)
- Assignment: Locate an editorial cartoon. Explain both the topic and the meaning of the cartoon, and write your own personal reaction to this cartoon in a journal entry.
- Read journal entries and write a response to every entry.

Personal Responsibilities

Curriculum Tie-in: Social Studies

Elementary

- Introduce the term "democracy." Ask students to give examples of what this word means. Have one student find this word in a dictionary and read aloud the definitions.
- Discuss the rights citizens have in a democracy.
- Discuss the responsibilities citizens have in a democracy.
- Assign students to work in small groups to create murals explaining what "personal responsibility" in a democracy looks like.
- Videotape the students talking about their murals.
- Display the murals and show the video on the school news network.

Middle School

- Introduce the term "democracy."
- Discuss the rights citizens have in a democracy.
- Discuss the responsibilities citizens have in a democracy.
- Discuss this quote by Helen Keller:
    "I am only one; but still I am one. I cannot do everything, but still I can do something. I will not refuse to do the something I can do."
- Invite a speaker who will address this topic with the class (for example, a member of the League of Women Voters) and allow time for questions and answers.

High School

- Discussion: What is a democracy?
- Discuss this quote by Margaret Meade:
    "Never doubt that a small group of thoughtful, committed citizens can change the world. Indeed, it is the only thing that ever has."
- Have students research a country that does not have democracy.
- Assignment: Write a two-page essay comparing the responsibilities that citizens have in the United States and in the country that was researched. Explain why it takes more effort to live in a democracy.
- Select the best essay for publication in the school newspaper or Web page.

Name _____

Date _____

Summarize media message #1:

Review: _____

Reflect: _____

React: _____

Summarize media message #2:

Review: _____

Reflect: _____

React: _____

Summarize media message #3:

Review: _____

Reflect: _____

React: _____

Use the back of this paper for the rest of the assignment.

"I am a part of all that I have read."

- John Kieran

"Reading is to the mind what exercise is to the body."

- Sir Richard Steele

"When you read a classic, you do not see more in the book than you did before; you see more in **you** than there was before."

- Clifton Fadiman

"In a very real sense, people who read good literature have lived more than people who cannot or will not read ... It is not true that we have only one life to live; if we can read, we can live as many lives and as many kinds of lives as we wish."

- S. I. Hayakawa

"The man who does not read good books has no advantage over the man who can't read them."

- Mark Twain

"There is more treasure in books than in all the pirates' loot on Treasure Island ... and best of all, you can enjoy these riches every day of your life."

- Walt Disney

"No entertainment is so cheap as reading; nor any pleasure so lasting."

- Lady Mary Wortley Montagu

"Every man who knows how to read has it in his power to magnify himself, to multiply the ways in which he exists, to make his life full, significant and interesting."

- Aldous Huxley

"We read to know we are not alone."

- C.S. Lewis

"People believe almost anything they see in print."

- Charlotte, *Charlotte's Web*

CHAPTER SIX

WHAT IS THE IMPACT OF THE MESSAGE ON SOCIETY?

The mass media have become so intertwined with other aspects of our culture that it is difficult to separate the media from the culture itself. The goal of media literacy studies is for students to become critical thinkers about the media. We could say that students in elementary school will become detectives and that the older students will become budding sociologists. The more students examine the various media sources and the role those mass media play in their lives and in their culture, the more sophisticated they will become in their thinking.

It is imperative that students be able to step back and analyze, question, interpret, and evaluate the messages that inundate their culture. As healthy skeptics, students learn to draw conclusions, make inferences, predict the future, and judge the worth while they continue to function in the culture. The purpose of media literacy is not to create cynics or pessimists, but to empower students to live in the culture while constantly examining it. Perhaps the motto could be: "Live with one's eyes and mind open." Advertising, for instance, is seeping into all possible crevices and crannies of the culture, and sends messages to consume and conform. Many schools, for example, have set policies that allow placement of advertising within the schools in return for financial considerations. It is possible that within our students' lifetimes, public buildings, such as libraries, schools, and courts, will be filled with advertising and paid sponsorships. Students must consider what they think is best for their world before it is too late to undo such thorough penetration by advertising messages.

Preparations for state assessments and preparations for life are one and the same. Thinking must be foremost in all aspects of students' lives. Media literacy strategies in this book provoke students' opinions, evaluations, and decisions about what to accept in the culture. This chapter focuses on issues and skills that go beyond the routine daily decisions of children and teens. This set of activities is meant to cause dialogue and discourse about our society and its future.

Draw Conclusions

Students must take in information and events in their world and draw conclusions. This skill will enable them to reach beyond the obvious and stretch to new dimensions. Sometimes these conclusions are apparent, sometimes nebulous, sometimes controversial. In all cases the students must comprehend all they have seen, heard, or read and then produce their own ideas. This skill appears on all state assessments in one form or another. According to the *GrassRoots Taxonomy of Thinking Skills* drawing conclusions is one of the higher-level thinking strategies. As teachers and media specialists move students to these higher levels, they stretch their students to new heights.

Every day we are given the facts; the conclusions are ours to draw. Our conclusions then shape how we think about our society and our world. Students must be able to assimilate information, draw conclusions about the culture's messages, and think about the ramifications of those messages.

Make Inferences

To make inferences is more difficult than to draw conclusions. For example, if a student says, "I'm going to watch 'Seinfeld' tonight," one immediately draws the conclusion that his family owns a television set or at least has access to one. If that student says, "I can watch anything I want on TV," the inferences might be that: a) he has a television set in his bedroom, b) his parents are lenient regarding his television watching, or c) he is often home alone without supervision. There is not necessarily one correct inference without obtaining more details. The more information offered, the more accurate the inferences. There is some reasoning going on, and it is necessary to "connect the dots."

The role of the news media is to present information; inferences are left to the audience. Fox Network News has a slogan: "We report; you decide!" Fox Network News is saying that they do not editorialize; they merely deliver the facts. In that case, any conclusions drawn or inferences made to the news stories must be those of the viewers.

Standardized tests measure the ability of students to take presented facts and "leap" to conclusions or inferences based on those facts. Without experience with these skills, students will struggle. Students are not born critical thinkers. Such a level of thinking takes repeated practice, and media literacy training provides the necessary practice.

Predict

Based on certain events, facts, or ideas, it is often necessary to predict the future. This component of critical thinking is vital to success. Again, this is a "leap." Take what is known and speculate about what happens next. This is not a random guess as there is often a foreseeable pattern to follow.

"Read part of the story and predict the ending" is a common activity in schools. Through repetition and feedback, this skill improves. The prediction is based on what is already known and what seems like a reasonable conclusion. There are many other activities that teachers and media specialists can use to improve the ability to predict. The lessons in this section of the book are based on media messages and will be appealing to students.

Judge the Worth

Evaluation is the highest level in Bloom's Taxonomy. Judging the worth of some-thing is subjective but, to be of value, must be based on facts and circumstances. This skill has immeasurable value and lifelong implications and applications. As adults we must judge the worth of things around us every day. The defense or jus-tification comes from knowledge, not feelings. The more students can move away from emotions driving their decisions and can focus on information, the more valid their judgments will become.

The messages delivered by the mass media provide authentic opportunities for students to practice the skills involved in evaluation.

The activities in this chapter—draw conclusions, make inferences, predict, and judge the worth—cause students to extrapolate from the known to the unidentified. This is higher-level thinking and stretches students to move outside their familiar responses.

ACTIVITIES

Draw Conclusions

Curriculum Tie-in: Language Arts and English
Elementary

- Introduce the phrase, "draw conclusions," and give examples.
- Give students a few minutes to quietly study the clothes that the class members are wearing.
- Have students draw conclusions about what American elementary school students wear to school.
- Compile a list of their conclusions. Ask whether all students have to wear the items on the list, and whether there are exceptions.
- Review what it means to draw conclusions. Repeat this activity with other topics during the school year.

Middle School

- Collect grocery ad inserts from local or regional newspapers.
- Divide students into small groups and give each group a few grocery ad inserts.
- Discuss what the phrase, "draw conclusions," means. Have students give examples.
- Assignment: Look through the food ads. Based on just these ads, draw conclusions about the eating habits of the people in our country. Draw conclusions about what non-food items Americans buy at grocery stores.
- Have the groups share their ideas.

High School

- Discuss the phrase, "draw conclusions."
- Assignment: Visit a bookstore and write down all the items for sale that are not books. Make a list of the various genre of books that are featured in the store. Write down conclusions you can draw about items stocked in bookstores in the United States and Americans' book preferences.
- Share the results; compile a list of conclusions. Discuss each conclusion for agreements and disagreements.

Make Inferences

Curriculum Tie-in: Language Arts and English
Elementary

- Order a classroom set of newspapers.

- Give each student a copy of the same newspaper.
- Discuss "hard news" (facts) and "soft news" (opinions, reviews, advertising).
- Assignment: Look through your newspaper and determine how much of the paper is "hard news" and how much is "soft news."
- Lead a class discussion to make inferences about various reasons that people might have for buying newspapers.

Middle School

- Order a classroom set of newspapers.
- Give all students a copy of the same newspaper.
- Have students locate the "help wanted ads."
- Assignment: Select a job heading and read all of the ads in that section. Write down any inferences you can make about the background education or experience required to do this job.
- Help students share and discuss their findings.

High School

- Collect college brochures; create a list of college Web sites.
- Discuss what it means to make inferences.
- Assignment: Locate and study a college brochure or college Web site. Make inferences about the college's priorities and the type of students they are seeking for admission.
- Have students share their findings and explain their specific reasons for making their inferences.

Predict

Curriculum tie-in: Language Arts and English
Elementary

- Discuss the word, "predict," and give examples.
- Order a classroom set of newspapers.
- Give all students a copy of the same newspaper.
- Have students locate the weather page and study the weather pattern for the past few days, including temperature, precipitation, and wind.
- As a class make a prediction for tomorrow's weather based on their findings.
- The next day discuss whether their prediction was correct. List reasons why some weather predictions are wrong.

Middle School

- Discuss the word "predict"; have students give examples of what this word means.

- Explain what life in America in 1938 was like, including the dependence on radio for entertainment and news, and the fact that there was no television available.
- Have the class listen to the radio program, "War of the Worlds."
- Describe the reaction people had in 1938, because they did not know it was a radio drama.
- Discussion: Why weren't the creators of this drama able to predict this reaction from the audience? Would the same thing happen today?

High School

- Discuss television ratings and why they are important.
- Direct students to visit the Web site for the Nielsen ratings: <http://tv.yahoo.com/nielsen>
- Ask students to look through next week's *TV Guide*, and predict the prime time ratings winners for next week.
- During the next week's class session, return to the Nielsen Web site to see if their predictions were correct.
- Discussion: Are predictions always right? If not, why? Name some factors that can affect predictions.

Judge the Worth
Curriculum Tie-in: Information Literacy
Elementary

- Introduce the term, "judge the worth," and explain that people will sometimes disagree among themselves on judgments of worth.
- Distribute copies of the worksheet on page 82, Reproducible 6.1, "Judge the Worth of the Book."
- Assignment: Select and read one fiction book; complete the worksheet; turn it in.
- Discussion: What criteria did you use to "judge the worth" of the book? How could other people make different judgments? What is necessary to "judge the worth" of something? Give examples of situations when it is necessary to "judge the worth."
- Repeat this activity several times during the school year.

Middle School

- Ask students to bring in pictures of celebrities. Posters, photographs, or magazine covers are best. Display the pictures in the classroom or library.
- Explain the phrase, "judge the worth" (justify the importance).
- Compile a list of celebrities and display the list.

- Discussion: What are celebrities? What makes celebrities popular? Who is your favorite celebrity? Give some reasons. Did everyone choose the same favorite celebrity? Why not?
- Assignment: Select your favorite celebrity. Write a journal entry about him or her, and include:
    - What makes this person a celebrity?
    - Why is this celebrity your personal favorite?
    - Judge the worth of this celebrity.
    - Give reasons why this celebrity is important to you.
    - Give reasons why this celebrity is important to other people in the United States.
- Discussion: What is the difference between a celebrity and a hero? Why is it easier to judge the worth of a hero?

High School

- Discuss the recent financial settlements between major tobacco companies and the government. How was this money to be used?
- Assignment: Visit this Web site, <www.tobaccofreekids.org>, select a state to investigate at the "Tobacco Toll," and write down the state's statistics.
- Encourage students to share their findings.
- Assignment: In your journal, justify the worth of this Web site to students in the United States.
- Read and respond to journal entries.

Name _____

Date _____

Select and read a book and complete this worksheet.

Title: _____

Author: _____

Illustrator: _____

Publisher: _____

Copyright date: _____

Judge the worth of this book, with 1 = poor and 10 = terrific.

1   2   3   4   5   6   7   8   9   10

Write five reasons for your judgment. Use complete sentences.

1. _____

_____

2. _____

_____

3. _____

_____

4. _____

_____

5. _____

_____

CHAPTER SEVEN

MAKE A MESSAGE

Students as Creators

As students have become involved in the analysis of media messages, they have internalized a number of aspects of media production: purpose, target audience, format, content, word choice, images, and other components. At this point they are able to produce their own messages and are prepared to select the best from available media formats.

The creation of media messages can be integrated into any curriculum area from kindergarten through high school. Creating and producing new messages is an effective vehicle to get students personally connected to the curriculum's content, whether it is the study of the Revolutionary War, writing haiku poetry, or learning about environmental factors that affect city life.

Too many so-called "media" classes in middle school or high school jump right into production without spending time on the awareness, analysis, and reflection levels that are basic to media literacy. To merely give a student a video camera and assume she knows enough about such factors as objectives, composition, lighting, camera angles, and intended audience keeps that student from experiencing the satisfaction of developing a quality product. More important, students must have sufficient media literacy skills in place to comprehend why the message is necessary and what delivery system is best for the message, and to then assess the impact of that message on the intended audience. The quality of the final product is less significant than the learning that occurs while creating it.

Cooperative Learning

In the real world the process of creating media messages is accomplished by teams of specialists working together. Although some of the learning activities in this book have been intended for individuals working alone, small groups and entire classes will find that the development of media messages requires cooperation among the individuals involved. The creation of media messages may be the ideal manifestation of the cooperative learning strategy, wherein two or more students work together on a learning assignment or final project. The possibilities for applying a cooperative learning environment in the educational system have traditionally been limited by practical restraints on time and resources. The tasks of choosing the content, format, target audience, point of view, and other components, lend themselves to either an individual or a group activity. Decisions such as which print or electronic medium is to be used can be made by students, and the final product can be identified either by students or the instructor. Subsequent tasks involving the designing, developing, and distributing of the finished message can be the responsibility of groups of student workers.

Content: Using a Graphic Organizer

The first step in creating a media message is a brainstorming activity. Allow students sufficient time to consider a variety of ways to state the message they want to share. There are many types of graphic organizers available online as shown in Figure 7.1. The media specialist and teacher

Figure 7.1 Graphic Organizers

Graphic Organizers

Students are often encouraged to use graphic organizers as pre-writing tools. Different organizers are used for different kinds of writing. Some commonly used types include: chain of events, clustering, compare/contrast, continuum, problem/solution, storyboards, and Venn Diagrams.

The following Web sites are useful resources for locating graphic organizers.

Library of Graphic Organizers
<http://curry.edschool.virginia.edu/go/edis771/notes/graphicorganizers/graphic>

Index of Graphic Organizers
<www.graphic.org/goindex.html>

Student Graphic Organizers, Schools of California Online Resources for Education
<www.sdcoe.k12.ca.us/score/actbank/sorganiz.htm>

Teacher Graphic Organizers, Schools of California Online Resources for Education
<www.sdcoe.k12.ca.us/score/actbank/torganiz.htm>

North Central Regional Educational Laboratory
<www.ncrel.org/sdrs/areas/issues/students/learning/lr1grorg.htm>

Education Place Graphic Organizers
<www.eduplace.com/graphicorganizer>

TeAch-nology Graphic Organizer Makers
<http://teachers.teach-nology.com/web_tools/graphic_org>

Teacher Vision Graphic Organizers
<www.teachervision.fen.com/lesson-plans/lesson-6293.html?s2&detoured=1>

can introduce several types and allow students to select which one they will use. During the school year students should become familiar with a variety of graphic organizers.

Format

Some teachers or media specialists may feel that their resources are not adequate for guiding students through the process of creating media messages. It is not necessary to have such extraordinary resources as high-end production studios nor is it mandatory for them to be experienced in computer applications such as iMovie software on the Macintosh computer. These resources are beneficial but not necessary. Teachers or media specialists who lack computer access can have students produce a wide array of media messages in other formats. Figure 7.2 lists an assortment of products that represent end products of higher-level thinking.

Figure 7.2 Student Product Ideas

Student Product Ideas

The following list from Canada's *GrassRoots Taxonomy of Thinking Skills* is offered to broaden the choices for student products.

Example Product List: Products which can be used to demonstrate application of the Thinking Skills Framework

Advertisement	Debate	Graphic design	Museum exhibit
Annotated bibliography	Detailed illustration	Greeting card	Musical composition
Art gallery	Diary	Illustrated story	News report
Biography	Diorama	Journal	Pamphlet
Blueprint	Display	Labeled diagram	Pattern with instructions
Board game	Drama	Large scale drawing	Photo essay
Book cover	Dramatic monologue	Lecture	Picture dictionary
Bulletin board	Editorial	Letter	Poem
Card game	Essay	Letter to the editor	Poster
Chart	Experiment	Lesson	Reference file
Collage	Experiment log	Line drawing	PowerPoint presentation
Collection with illustration	Fact file	Magazine article	Survey
Collection with narrative	Fairy tale	Map	Transparency of overhead
Comic strip	Fable	Map with legend	Vocabulary list
Computer program	Family tree	Mobile	Written report
Crossword puzzle	Glossary graph	Monograph	

Used with permission, The GrassRoots Program, Canada's SchoolNet.
part of the Canadian Ministry of Industry (Industry Canada)
<www.schoolnet.ca/grassroots/e/project.centre/shared/taxonomy.asp>

The *GrassRoots Taxonomy of Thinking Skills* shows that the process of creating is a higher-level activity. To produce a media message, students move beyond lower levels of critical thinking to the levels of synthesis or evaluation. As students complete their products, they have gained a wealth of knowledge and at the same time have honed their thinking skills.

The complexity of the selected format might be determined by access to, or ability to use, various media. Consider this scenario: After lessons on fact vs. opinion, the art teacher wants the students to create clay mugs that include messages, but a kiln is not available. The students' messages might be created on paper instead. The format is not as important as the active leaning that occurs and the critical thinking steps required to make the message. *Hyper Studio* and *Power Point* are valuable tools for students to use, but access to computers and availability of time to complete projects might prohibit the use of this software. It is important to focus on the process of learning more than on the product.

Not all of the student-created media products listed in the graphic in Figure 7.2 will be directly applicable to items on state assessments. However, they are worthwhile and legitimate results of learned skills, authentic tasks that can instigate student involvement with the mass media in life-changing ways. For example, after studying editorial cartoons, students who become directly involved in the production of original cartoons are likely to seek out and analyze editorial cartoons whenever they read newspapers. Furthermore, their ability to deconstruct and analyze these opinion-based drawings will transfer to similar situations, such as test questions on state assessments.

Design and development of the end product causes students to consider the specific content needed to get their message across, the best format for their message, and the impact this product will have on their target audience. For example, a group of students has decided to create a message about the health concerns associated with chewing tobacco (content). If they select a poster as the desired medium (format), the following are some decisions that must be made: size and color of the font, images, background, and intended audience. In order to reach the target audience, students can decide to place the poster in a conspicuous location such as on a wall in the school cafeteria for other students to see.

One tool located on page 90 to help students with production strategies is Reproducible 7.2, "Create a Storyboard." Assign students to work in small groups to create 30-second skits or television commercials. Distribute copies of the worksheet to students so they can develop storyboards for their projects. Take time to review the storyboards before the skits or commercials are started to ensure that students are on the right track.

Assessing the Impact

The impact of any media message is heavily dependent on the format in which it appears. Consider the "two second rule" for billboards. Because of that rule, creators of effective billboards select a minimum of text and large images, graphics, and recognizable icons because drivers in passing cars must take in and process the messages quickly. As students become knowledgeable about the impact that media messages have on them and their culture, they better understand the time, energy, and money that are consumed in creating effective media messages. They recognize that every aspect of every successful media message demands extensive preparation and planning.

Students design the message, determine the format the message will have, create and distribute it, and then assess its impact. This strategy may be new territory for most students. They may have created messages in classes before, but perhaps without the breadth of understanding they now have. At this stage they must reflect on the audience the message was meant to reach and decide whether the message did, indeed, make an impression. They can measure the effectiveness of their messages in several ways. Some measures they can use are to conduct a survey, orally interview some intended audience members, and gather written feedback via e-mail or letters from those who have seen, read, or heard the message. Keep in mind that this procedure is not an exact science. At best they will get only a sampling of the total impact. The influence of a message or product on an audience is short-lived, relatively unreliable, and sometimes emotional. This assessment is a valuable learning experience, however, and some means of determining the effectiveness of the message must be included in the project.

Once these tasks have been completed, the students should take time to reflect on the process, perhaps in their media journals. The introspective part of the project causes students to better understand the purpose of the activity. Parents can also be involved at this point by being invited to visit the school to view the completed projects. They will become informed about these media literacy activities while at the same time supplying positive reinforcement for the students.

An extension of this media project can be the emergence of a student news bureau for the school. With minimal equipment students can create and produce a news program to be aired over the school's closed circuit system or the community access television channel.

Software is available to aid in the creation of media products. One example is the "Between the Lines" media literacy product available from Tyndal Stone Media in Canada. By using "Between the Lines," students are able to choose from eight diverse media projects, such as creating a music video and designing a public service announcement. The "Decisions, Decisions" curriculum kits from Tom Snyder Productions include CD-ROMs, videos, and activities. Some of the timely topics include "Violence in the Media," "Substance Abuse," and "On the Campaign Trail." The units are aimed at middle-school and high-school students and require students to take on the role of media decision-makers. These role-playing opportunities allow students to better comprehend the responsibilities of

Figure 7.3 News in the Making

News in the Making

One way to motivate students after they understand media literacy strategies is to create a student news bureau at the school. This could be a weekly news program. A daily program is difficult to maintain and soon follows a routine of announcements, which tends to stifle creativity. Some schools allow students to create a news program during their educational day, while others use lunch, recess, or before or after school time.

Bringing news into the daily lives of students is important and can develop into a habit. Look to "CNN Student News" on the CNN cable channel for a program geared to students. The short and meaningful program is aired during the night and is meant to be taped and then used whenever it fits into the school day. The daily program selects news stories that broaden students' understanding of the world around them. Information about the Monday-Friday program and additional resources can be found at <http://cnnstudentnews.cnn.com/fyi/index.html>

A journalism curriculum for high-school students is offered through CNN Student News and is designed to teach the basics of news reporting. This curriculum can be found at <www.learning.turner.com/cnnstudentnewsjc/curriculum.shtml>

Adobe Digital Kids Club at <www.adobe.com/education/digkids> offers tips and information about using digital cameras to report the news and create multimedia programs. Teachers and media specialists can find lessons and activities at <www.adobe.com/education/digkids/lessons/main.html> The use of digital cameras can bring authenticity and enthusiasm to student video projects.

gatekeepers and to get more critical thinking practice than might otherwise be available to them.

Career Education

As students finalize their projects they will become more involved in the total atmosphere of the mass media and perhaps in some related careers. The teacher or media specialist could provide a bulletin board for students to post a compilation of media-related careers. As new ideas are suggested they should be added to the list. Assign students to investigate opportunities in related vocations and report them to the class.

After the media projects have been finalized, field trips to media outlets such as radio or television stations would be meaningful. The educational advantages are unlimited and can be augmented by having speakers from advertising or public relations firms or other media-related businesses visit classes. Interactions by the students with the members of the media community can cement relationships and reinforce the learning. Students can ask questions and investigate career opportunities.

Students are empowered when they make their own media messages. Distribute copies of Reproducible 7.1, "Design, Develop, and Distribute the Message" on page 89, as a planning instrument for student projects. One activity might be to have students design a logo or slogan for the class, library, or school. A contest could follow to allow the class or entire student body to select the winner. Then the winning logo or slogan could be placed on the school Web site and on banners, stationery, and clothing such as T-shirts, sweatshirts, or hats.

The goal of improving realism in our schools will clearly have been realized. In either the individual or group mode, students seem to enjoy learning when they create authentic messages. The final media product is a clear demonstration of a complex set of knowledges and skills attained by the participating students. Students will never forget the experience and will remain media-savvy because the developed skills will continue to be applied throughout their lives.

Name(s) _____

Date _____

Designing, developing, and distributing a media message takes a great deal of planning. Use this worksheet as a master plan for the entire project.

Content: _____

_____

_____

Purpose: _____

_____

_____

Point of View: _____

_____

_____

Format: _____

_____

_____

Target Audience: _____

_____

_____

Where to place the message (hallway, school newspaper): _____

_____

_____

Method to assess impact: _____

_____

_____

What was learned during this project: _____

_____

Annapolis High School
Media Center

Name(s) _____

Date _____

A storyboard is a graphic, sequential depiction of a narrative. It includes the script and production notes. It is used to design a commercial, television news program, Web site, story, or other type of production.

Select a topic for a 30-second skit or television commercial and use the worksheet to develop the scenes and script. Include all production notes.

	Drawing	Script or Production notes
Scene 1		
Scene 2		
Scene 3		
Scene 4		

CHAPTER EIGHT

APPLYING CRITICAL THINKING

Relevance

Perhaps the most frequent criticism of curricula in today's schools is the seeming lack of relevance to today's culture. For students to get involved in a learning activity they must recognize the relevance of the content to their personal lives and once they do, learning will proceed. On the other hand, subject matter that appears to have no bearing on their individual lives seems to be a waste of time and effort, and often students do not see any reason to be involved. This reaction is certainly not a reason to dismiss the existing curricula, but is strong support for merging media literacy lessons into them.

One media literacy lesson may not change a life, but a series of well-constructed, practical, thoughtfully-sequenced activities that involve students in the study of media messages allows them to see the contemporary culture as important and worth studying. Dismissing today's world as "their culture" and not embracing it as worthy of examination sends a loud and clear message to students that the "world of school" is obsolete, impractical, and superfluous.

The ultimate goal of teaching students to use the review, reflect, and react formula in dealing with messages of the mass media is to enable them to acquire critical thinking skills, ones they will find applicable to their entire lives.

The more opportunities K-12 students have to learn information and skills that are useful in their daily lives, the more school will be deemed worthwhile. Certainly the study of past cultures, social studies, and other traditional subjects should not be purged. However, there are ways to integrate media literacy into any subject at any time, and in most instances this approach will help to make the subject matter come alive without extending the existing curriculum.

Media messages have so completely saturated our culture that students and adults often accept them without any contemplation about how different life would be without them. Media literacy lessons cause students to look at their society through new eyes and gain insights into popular culture. In the study of media literacy, students get enlarged views of their world—views that extend beyond the learning outcomes that were envisioned by teachers, media specialists, and curriculum planners.

A realistic example of this aspect of media literacy in education can be seen as students study the role of newspapers in our society. Most students feel print news sources are pointless because of the multitude of electronic news sources available. The long-term impact of the newspaper activities that follow is significant. In one lesson, students dissect the "hard" news and "soft" news found in a newspaper. In another they study the opinion pieces, such as editorials, editorial cartoons, reviews, and letters to the editor. In still another they examine the various styles of advertising found in newspapers. Another activity causes students to investigate countries that do not have a free press while others compare and contrast the news stories found in newspapers and television news programs. Students read newspapers and select news stories that illustrate how the mass media shape culture. Elementary students compile a list of features found in a newspaper and share that information with parents at a PTA meeting. Middle school students trace the history of newspapers and create a timeline. High school students examine the local newspaper to discover what is left out and discuss possible reasons for such omissions. Another class learns about the newspaper format in order to create their own class newspaper. Others discuss photojournalism and investigative reporting as career choices. A special education class makes a list of how newspapers can help them. Another group analyzes photographs found on the front pages of the newspapers and draws conclusions about their purpose and selection. A high school class scrutinizes tabloid newspapers and reports on their findings. After completing these lessons, students are ready to think critically and realistically about the question, "Are newspapers still valuable in today's society?"

When schools integrate media literacy into their curricula, one outcome will likely be that the students develop a broader understanding of how the free enterprise system works and the role of the mass media in a democratic form of government. They may discover that there can be no democracy without media outlets that are free to independently gather and report news, and there can be no free media system without a democratic government, a fundamental civics lesson.

The upshot of all media literacy lessons is that students will no longer be nonchalant about the messages they see, hear, or read. They become active consumers of media messages rather than merely passive spectators. Even more important, they become neither sponges nor cynics but develop into healthy skeptics. That is the goal of media literacy.

What About Those Tests?

In preparation for upcoming standardized tests, which all students must take to disclose the extent of their learning, educators attempt to fit every skill and fact they can into the school days preceding the "big event." Results of the tests are often interpreted to reflect on the educators' performance, so there is a concerted effort to allow nothing to interfere with filling students with the specific materials they will need to answer test questions. Often, however, the "extras" that are discarded to make room for the so-called "test preparation" are the very activities students enjoy and crave—the authentic and pleasurable aspects of learning. These activities might be plays or skits, stories that are read aloud, nature walks, service opportunities, field trips, performances, research projects, fine arts events, and so on. As the accountability noose tightens, school boards and administrators often minimize the most meaningful parts of the school day by removing what are considered unnecessary "extras." With tunnel vision focused solely on test scores, they may find they have a school that is devoid of creativity, enthusiasm, and relevance to students.

Standardized tests are opportunities for students to shine. As they embrace learning, grow intellectually, and begin to think critically about everything, they will develop the self-confidence to do well on assessments. These tests will then not be feared but welcomed. School should be thought of not as preparation for state assessments but as preparation for life.

Collaboration

As media specialists and teachers collaborate to develop meaningful and practical media-related lessons, students will benefit and soon will consider school to be surprisingly relevant and exciting. The bridge from school to culture will be apparent to them. This change in attitude is especially likely to happen when the strengths and personalities of the collaboration team members are combined to guide the selection of activities, strategies, and end products.

Teachers and media specialists know their students and know the curriculum. Now it is time to "think outside the school building" to connect learning within the school to the world outside beyond the playground. Bringing authentic media messages into daily schoolroom lessons makes learning real and motivating. The introduction of such objects as cereal boxes, magazine covers, and messages on clothing as content to be studied sparks the attention of students. The more dynamic the exchange of ideas, the more involved students will be in their learning.

The list of suggested activities and curriculum connections in this chapter is meant to further the collaboration process but is not all-inclusive. There is no limit to the ways that media literacy can be incorporated into existing curricula. As media messages are interwoven into every curriculum area, students will transfer thinking into the myriad of media messages in their lives.

The transfer of critical thinking has always been an issue in education. If a student learns to decipher and solve story problems in math class, for example, will she then be able to take real-life mathematical situations and apply those skills she learned at school? Not necessarily. Schools are so departmentalized that often the skills and knowledge acquired during the classes within a school day don't seem to carry over to the "big picture"—the daily lives of students outside the school. However, in the activities described below, the world of the culture around the students is brought into the school to provide a practical basis for learning activities. These lessons extend the thinking beyond the classes at school to the actual culture students live in.

The transfer of critical thinking required in these lessons to the state assessments is facilitated when critical thinking is part of all daily lessons rather than a separate subject. The media messages are merely the opportunity or motivation for students to contemplate in new ways the world around them. Instead of merely learning the facts about the early exploration of America by Europeans, for example, the class might compare and contrast communication methods then and now. From these findings they might draw conclusions about the inherent problems those explorers had compared to today's explorers in their travel into space. Rather than remaining at the knowledge level of Bloom's Taxonomy of Thinking, students become involved in higher-level thinking, while analyzing their culture's communication modes. The lesson in this way becomes relevant to their lives and will stay with them longer than mere facts. By embracing media literacy within all lessons, educators enable students to gain more than knowledge and develop into conscious and aware thinkers, always alert to the larger picture. When state assessments require them to think in new ways about new topics, they will be ready.

The following compilation of ideas for quick media literacy lessons is meant to supplement the activities in previous chapters. As the collaboration process triggers new ideas, add them to the list. Users of this book should write in it and use it as a reference.

Additional Media Literacy Lessons

Math

- Create a bulletin board called "Math is all around us!" Put a large circle in the center. Assign students to bring in examples of the use of math in newspapers, ads, or magazines, and place them in the circle until it is filled. Discuss how much math is part of their world. Share this bulletin board with parents or with other classes.
- Use television program listings, such as the *TV Guide*, to create math problems for an assignment. Problems can be based on lengths of some listed programs and total time consumed by or between selected programs. Use this math assignment as a springboard for a discussion about television and reasons that specific programs air at certain times of the day.
- Discuss the costs involved in creating television programs. Find out how much 30 seconds of "air time" at a local television channel

costs and share this information with students. Have students count the number of 30-second ads that are part of a half-hour program and then calculate the total amount paid for "air time" during that program. Discuss how television stations use this money (to purchase the program, personnel costs, equipment).

- Use classified ads from a newspaper as the focus of a lesson on money. Learn how much a classified ad in the local paper costs. Have students select several ads from their favorite categories and calculate how much those ads cost. Discuss the purpose of classified ads.
- Have each student bring in a chart, a graph, or some statistics from a news magazine or newspaper. Participants are to summarize their findings and share them with the class. Display the math formats and the summaries.
- Videotape a math-based television program and show it to the class, pausing often for discussion. Ask students to apply what they have learned to situations in their lives.
- Tell students to select a current or former hit movie. Learn from the movie's Web site how much the movie cost to make, and determine how much the movie has taken in from box office revenues. Calculate whether the movie was a financial success.
- Assign students the task of finding out how much one copy of the local newspaper costs. List all the costs involved in the making of that newspaper, such as personnel, paper, ink, machinery, building expenses, distribution. Brainstorm about how these expenses are paid.
- Discuss election campaigns and how candidates pay for their campaigns. Talk about whether there should be limits on how much money candidates can spend or whether richer candidates should have more opportunities to "spread the word" than less wealthy candidates.
- Introduce the concept of public broadcasting versus commercial broadcasting on television and radio. Have students investigate how programs are funded on public broadcasting channels and stations.

Language Arts and Information Literacy

- Have students focus on the media messages that are part of their lives. Use Reproducible 8.1, "Messages Are Everywhere!" on page 101 as an assignment to start the process. Discussion about their findings will raise awareness of the saturation of society by media messages.
- Invite a local author or illustrator to the class to enlighten the students about the publishing process.
- Discuss popular movies that depict teenagers. Discuss common stereotypes about teenagers and stereotypes in general. List some negative consequences of stereotypes.
- Direct students to learn how to use the Flesch-Kincaid readability level feature in Microsoft Word software in order to establish the grade level of their writing. Then ask them to rewrite their work to increase the grade level.

- Locate a teacher from another state or another country and set up student pen pals. Have students use traditional mail or e-mail to correspond with those students.
- Have students locate messages on their clothing. Discuss why advertising messages on clothes are not only acceptable but popular.
- Media literacy can be used in journalism classes when teaching about news, production techniques, and editing. Ask: How has the maxim "If it bleeds, it leads" changed the look of news broadcasts? What are some alternatives to this approach?
- Students can write scripts for television or radio dramas, ads, news programs, or editorials.
- Direct students to create new covers for "ugly" books in the library. The covers need to capture the attention of the target audience (students).
- Instruct students to research the Newbery, Caldecott, Coretta Scott King, and other book awards. The American Library Association Web site lists many book awards at <www.ala.org>. Each student selects one book that should be nominated for one of these awards and defends the choice, either orally or in writing.
- Discuss what makes a book a classic. Ask, "Do you think the Harry Potter books will still be on library shelves 50 years from now?" Students must give thoughtful reasons for their answers.
- Have students consider this scenario: A new school is being built, and there is not enough money for both hardcover and paperback library books. Students are to list several factors that must be weighed in the decision whether to buy fewer of the longer-lasting hardcover books or more of the less durable paperbacks.
- Introduce the concept of movies as literature. Discuss books that have been made into movies. Distribute copies of Reproducible 8.2, "Movies as Literature" on page 102, and give the students a week to complete the assignment. Follow up with discussions about whether the movies should be considered to be types of literature.
- Remind students of the axiom, "You can't judge a book by its cover." Have them locate and think about magazine covers. Assign the Reproducible 8.3 "Compare and Contrast," on page 103, as homework for the students. Create a display of magazine covers after the assignment has been completed.
- Assign each student to read a book of poetry. They are to create an original poem about something in their culture they feel strongly about.
- Subscribe to a classroom set of newspapers or ask students to bring in newspapers from home. Use Reproducible 8.4 "Examine a News Story" on page 104, as an assignment to trigger thinking about news stories. Use this worksheet several times throughout the school year to reinforce the "Five Ws and an H" strategy.
- Ask: "Is reading still necessary?" Discuss this question. Follow up with Reproducible 8.5 "Why Read?" Survey on page 105, and have students share their findings.

Social Studies

- Students select a country other than the United States to research how the lifestyles of students their age in that country differ from their own. For example, find out how students spend their leisure time and money.
- Display the covers of news magazines, such as *Time for Kids*, *Weekly Reader*, *Time,* or *Newsweek*. Students then work in small groups to nominate one person who should be considered for the cover. Students are then to justify their suggestions.
- Have students locate, cut out, and study editorial cartoons or political cartoons. Use Reproducible 8.6 "Editorial Cartoons" on page 106, as a worksheet for students to complete. Follow up with a discussion about the impact of editorial cartoonists.
- Direct students to brainstorm about what life was like 100 years ago in their town or city. Have them compare and contrast life now and then by depicting both eras in two drawings. They then share their drawings with the class.
- Have students predict what life will be like 100 years from now in their town and city and write a descriptive piece about their predictions. Ask them to share predictions with the class.
- Discuss the lead or cover stories in newspapers, news magazines, and television news programs. Review the concept of gatekeepers. Use Reproducible 8.7 "The Lead Story" on page 107, as an assignment for the students. Have them share their ideas.
- Help students create, produce, and videotape a weekly current events news program and air it over the school's television network.
- Discuss what a democracy is. Together students should create a list of specific characteristics of life in a democracy. Instruct students to respond in their journals to the question, "Do you think every country should be a democracy?" and to justify their ideas.
- Assign students to read the Bill of Rights, rewrite the document in current language, and share their versions with younger students.
- Introduce the term "jolt" (see Glossary on page 111). Discuss why jolts are part of today's entertainment and are used in commercials, television programs, and movies.
- One component of social studies is the study of contemporary society. Discuss infomercials as a reflection of society. Have students complete Reproducible 8.8 "Infomercials" on page 108, and compare their results. Ask: What does this tell you about our society?

Health and Physical Education

- Students research the health risks involved in getting tattoos on their bodies. Ask them to create media messages to share the information with others.
- Help students promote a "Let's Get Physical" day at school with contests, sponsors, prizes, and media coverage.
- Direct each student to create a 30-second, health-related message.

Allow one student each day to share the new message with the rest of the school over the public address system.

- Students investigate what the word "calorie" means. Tell students to use the Internet to research the proper daily calorie count for themselves, based on age, size, weight, and height. Instruct students to keep a log of the food they consume during one week and then calculate their average calorie intake each day. Ask students to draw conclusions about their diet.
- Discuss famous athletes and what makes some athletes more popular than others. Students are to select their favorite athletes, bring to class photos of the athletes, and explain to the class reasons for their selections. Display the photos.
- Have students bring in "warning" labels that appear on food items, cigarette packages, and equipment. Read these together and discuss the consequences of use as stated on the warnings.
- Sports have become a major type of entertainment. The commercials aired during sports programs on television target specific audiences. Have students complete Reproducible 8.9 "Sports Sponsors" on page 109, and discuss their findings. Ask: What did you learn from this assignment?

Science

- Create a bulletin board for science articles. Students locate news items about science, read them, summarize them in writing, and then place the articles on the bulletin board so others can read them.
- Assign students to videotape a lab experiment, explaining what is happening as they proceed. They then share the videotape over the school's television network.
- Help students predict some specific things scientists will learn or be able to do in the next 50 years.
- Have students each learn about one current scientist who is making a difference. Each is to create a poster about the scientist, and all the posters are to be displayed in the science hall or cafeteria.

History

- Introduce a lesson about slogans. Have students create specific slogans for people they are studying in history lessons. One example can be slogans for the British soldiers and American patriots during the Revolutionary War. Display the slogans under a flag of the selected country or group.
- Direct students to watch television news programs and reflect on the formulas and formats (e.g., the number and position of anchors, the time allocated to weather and sports) that are used to broadcast the news. Students then create a news program about the period of history they are studying, with anchors, reporters, weathermen, and sportscasters. They then share their program with the school during an assembly or performances in classrooms.

- Students read biographies of famous people from the specific time period they are studying. They dress up as the famous people they read about and give reports about "their lives" to the class. Videotape the performances to share with other classes or parents.
- Discuss how people who live 100 years from now will remember this time period. Have students bring in newspaper headlines representing people or events that will be remembered and display them in the library or classroom.
- Discuss: What was the most important invention in the past 50 years? Have students justify all suggestions. Vote to select the one that was the most important.
- Heroes are part of history. Lead a discussion about the heroes of today. Distribute copies of Reproducible 8.10 "Who Is Your Hero?" survey on page 110, and give students one week to complete this assignment. Discuss their findings. Then ask students to write an essay about their personal heroes.

Art

- Take a field trip to an art museum and have students compare and contrast the impact that various art media have on them as individuals.
- Each student researches facts about one artist's life and style. Then each student creates a drawing, painting, sculpture, or other art medium in that artist's style. Students share with the class the resulting artwork and accumulated information about the artists.
- Discuss advertising. Throughout the school year have students bring in examples of print ads. Display them on the wall and assign students to deconstruct the ads as time allows. See Reproducible 3.2 "Components of a Media Message" on page 47.
- Begin each class by showing a new piece of art. Have students discuss the point of view of the artist.
- Introduce illustrations as an art form. Ask students to select and read one picture book from the library and complete an analysis about the book. Use Reproducible 2.4 "4 Part Analysis" on page 30.
- Discuss graffiti as art. Ask whether artists should be allowed to put graffiti on public buildings. What are some suggestions to allow these artists to be creative without defacing others' property?
- Introduce logos and share a number of popular company, team, and school logos. Help students create personal logos to use on their stationery, notebooks, or T-shirts.
- Using butcher paper, create a display in the hall with the question: What is art? Urge students, teachers, staff members, and parents to add their thoughts. Instruct students to read and reflect on the answers.
- Introduce the concept of storyboards. Have students create storyboards about a school news story. If time is available, have the students produce news stories from their storyboards and videotape

them. These can be shared with other classes or aired over the school television network. Use "Reproducible 7.2: Create a Storyboard" on page 90.

Music

- Videotape national news programs and have students listen to the opening music for each program. Assign the students to create original 10-second opening music for the school news program.
- Introduce music used in television commercials as a topic for study. Videotape commercials and show one to the class each day. Discuss the background music. Emphasize that it is composed and performed by real live musicians. Invite a local musician to the class to discuss music (especially for commercials) as a career possibility for students.
- Give students the opportunity to create original music for poems they have written. Encourage them to share their compositions and poems with other classes.
- Have students research a current or historical popular American music style, such as jazz, swing, reggae, rock, blues, or hip hop. Allow the students to choose a format through which they will communicate their findings to the class or school.
- Discuss popular music. Direct students to generate reasons why some music "catches on" and some disappears without popularity. Compile a class list of reasons given by students about this topic; display the list and add new ideas during the school year.
- Introduce jingles as a music format. Discuss "hot" topics in the current culture, such as popular videogames, celebrities, or movies that seem to be candidates for use of jingles. Help students create original 10-second jingles about these events, items, or people.

NOTE: These lessons can be used as stated, modified, or completely revamped, depending on the ideas of the teacher and media specialist, circumstances, curriculum, time limitations, and students' interests, needs, and abilities.

The Next Steps

The glossary includes media literacy terms that may be new to students or even to teachers or media specialists. These words can be introduced in the context of the activities offered in this book or as vocabulary words in language arts and English classes.

The resources listed in the Appendix will help guide educators to Web sites, books, videos, kits, and organizations to further the fusion of media literacy into daily classroom activities.

The more media literacy, that is, critical thinking about all media messages, becomes commonplace in the daily lives of students, the more ready they will be for state assessments, and the more prepared they will be for their roles as citizens in a democracy.

Name _____

Date _____

Take time to observe the world around you. Write down the format, a brief statement of the content, and the location of at least 20 messages. An example is given.

	Format	Content	Location
	billboard	cigarette advertisement	Highway 7
1.			
2.			
3.			
4.			
5.			
6.			
7.			
8.			
9.			
10.			
11.			
12.			
13.			

Use the back of this paper to continue the list.

Name _____

Date _____

Movies can often have a major impact on society in the same way literature can. In fact, some of the same elements are found in movies, such as theme, setting, plot, and main characters.

Select and watch a movie that you consider to be significant. The movie can be viewed at a movie theater, on television, or as a video/DVD rental. Then use complete sentences to answer these questions.

What is the name of the movie? (**title**) _____

_____

_____

Who were the main **characters**? _____

_____

_____

Where is the **setting**? _____

_____

_____

Summarize the storyline. (**plot**) _____

_____

_____

What was the **conflict** in the story? _____

_____

_____

What was the **theme** or **genre** of the movie? _____

_____

_____

Why do you think this movie is noteworthy? List specific reasons why this movie should be watched by others. Use the back of this paper for your answer.

Name _____

Date _____

Often magazine covers are merely variations on a theme. Select and examine two issues of the same magazine. Answer the questions based on your findings.

What is the name of the magazine? _____

_____

What are the issue dates? _____

_____

Compare the magazine covers. List all the features that are the same. _____

_____

_____

_____

_____

Contrast the magazine covers. List all the features that are different. _____

_____

_____

_____

_____

Based on the covers, draw conclusions about this magazine, including purpose, target audience, format, and content. Use the back of this paper for your answers.

Name _____

Date _____

Select, cut out, and read a news story from a print source, such as a newspaper or news magazine. Answer the following questions about the news item, and then staple the news article to this paper.

Who is the news story about? _____

_____

_____

What happened? _____

_____

_____

Where did this take place? _____

_____

_____

When did this take place? _____

_____

_____

Why is this news story important? _____

_____

_____

How did it happen? _____

_____

_____

What is your personal reaction to this news? Use the back of this paper for your answer.

Name _____

Date _____

Select 5-10 adults and ask them the question, "Why read?" List their names and summarize their responses below. Use the back of this paper for additional responses.

Adult #1: _____

_____

_____

_____

Adult #2: _____

_____

_____

_____

Adult #3: _____

_____

_____

_____

Adult #4: _____

_____

_____

_____

Adult #5: _____

_____

_____

_____

Name _____

Date _____

Editorial and political cartoons capsulize an opinion about an issue or candidate in one or two frames.

Locate, cut out, and "read" an editorial or political cartoon. Answer the questions in complete sentences based on the cartoon's information. Use the back of this paper, if necessary. Staple the cartoon to this paper.

What issue or candidate is the cartoon addressing? _____

_____

_____

_____

What background, clothing, or props does the artist use to give you additional information? _____

_____

_____

_____

What information do you need to know for this cartoon to be meaningful? _____

_____

_____

_____

What is the point of view of the artist? _____

_____

_____

_____

Do you agree with the artist's point of view? Give reasons for your answer.
Use the back of this paper for your answer.

Name _____

Date _____

The lead or cover story receives that prominent placement to catch the attention of the reader or viewer.

Select a current newspaper or news magazine, or view a television news program. Examine the lead or cover news story and complete the worksheet.

Summarize the lead or cover story: _____

_____

_____

_____

_____

_____

_____

Why would this story be of interest to readers or viewers? _____

_____

_____

_____

_____

_____

_____

Justify the placement of this news story or select another news story that you find more important and defend your choice as more appropriate for the lead or cover. Use the back of this paper for your answer.

Name _____

Date _____

"Infomercial" is a word that has recently been added to our vocabulary. It is an information-based commercial that is usually 30 minutes in length. The sponsor purchases air time for the infomercial. It is not regular television programming.

Select and watch an infomercial. Answer the following questions, using complete sentences.

What product was being sold? _____

_____

_____

Who was the target audience for the infomercial? _____

_____

_____

What person, such as a celebrity, a doctor, or an athlete, was used to sell the product? _____

_____

_____

What method was used to capture the attention of the audience? _____

_____

_____

What was your personal reaction? _____

_____

_____

Why do you think people watch infomercials? _____

_____

_____

Name _____

Date _____

Sports programs appeal to a very specific target audience. Knowing that, advertisers buy air time to reach those people.

Watch a football, basketball, baseball, or hockey game on television. During the game, list categories for all of the sponsors of that game, and then answer the questions. Use the back of this page, if necessary.

Sports program: _____

_____

_____

_____

Date and time of sports event: _____

_____

_____

Categories of the sponsors: _____

_____

_____

_____

_____

Based on the advertisements, what conclusions can you draw about the target audience of this sports program? _____

_____

_____

_____

_____

_____

Name _____

Date _____

Heroes are people who make positive impressions on our lives.

Select 5-10 adults who are important in your life and ask them to tell you about their personal heroes. Record your notes on this paper. Use the back of this paper for additional responses.

Adult #1: _____

_____

_____

_____

Adult #2: _____

_____

_____

_____

Adult #3: _____

_____

_____

_____

Adult #4: _____

_____

_____

_____

Adult #5: _____

_____

_____

GLOSSARY

air time Radio or television time purchased by advertisers to promote products. For example a television station might sell eight minutes of air time during a 30-minute sitcom to help defray the cost of the television program, and also to help pay for other expenses such as personnel, their building, equipment, and satellite dishes. The cost of a 30-second segment of television air time varies based on the popularity of the television program.

audience The people who receive the message.

bias An unfair preference or dislike of something or someone.

celebrity endorsement The use of a well-known person, animal, or cartoon character to be the spokesperson for a product in an advertisement.

construct To create a media message in which each element has an intentional purpose, point of view, format, and target audience.

content The words, images, characters, and information within a message.

deconstruct To take apart; to analyze the individual parts to better understand the whole.

demographics The statistical characteristics of human populations, such as age or income, used especially to identify markets for television sponsors.

documentary A type of film or television program that provides information. A documentary is recognized by its style, tone, and voice to be different from entertainment programming.

editing The act of splicing or putting together film or videotape clips in order to create a television commercial, program, or movie.

format The style or delivery mechanism, such as a comic strip, magazine ad, or television commercial, used to distribute a message.

gatekeeper An individual or group that controls the flow of information or entertainment. The gatekeeper can select, delete, prioritize, ignore, or reorganize information. The managing editor of a newspaper is a gatekeeper.

genre One of the categories of artistic, musical, or literary work, grouped on the basis of form, style, or subject matter. Fairy tales are a genre of literature.

glamorize To make something appear more attractive than it really is.

hard news The facts or data involved in a news story. An example would be the "who, what, where, when, and how" information in a news item.

icon An easily-recognized symbol that represents a company, product, or other item.

infomercial A video or audio format that combines information and commercials. Air time is purchased on television and radio to promote products through infomercials. It is not regular television programming.

jingle A catchy tune or verse that is used to sell a product.

jolt Humor, sexual scenes, action, or other intentional means of keeping the viewer actively involved in the television program, commercial, music video, or movie.

mass media Communications formats that use technology and are capable of reaching a mass of people simultaneously.

media diet The sum total of all the media in one's daily life including television, radio, CDs, books, magazines, and the Internet.

media literacy The application of critical thinking to the messages of the mass media. Media literacy is the ability to access, analyze, interpret, evaluate, and communicate messages in a variety of forms.

medium A communications format, such as an e-mail, poster, or letter.

movie trailers The name given to the coming attractions or teasers that include segments from an upcoming movie. The purpose is to attract viewers to a new movie that is about to be released.

news magazine A term that refers to a weekly print magazine or television program that summarizes and analyzes the news.

Newspapers in Education (NIE) The department of a newspaper that serves educators by offering curricula and services. Teachers may arrange to have multiple copies of the newspaper delivered for classroom use by contacting this department.

parody A literary, television, or musical work in which the style of an author, program, or written work is closely imitated for comic effect or ridicule.

peer pressure The influence by peers on the way one thinks, speaks, dresses, and behaves. Peer pressure can be positive or negative.

point of view (POV) The way in which one looks at subject matter. In television, movies, and photography, point of view is the perspective from which the production is shot.

pop culture The totality of widely popular media products such as music, mass market books, prime time television shows, movies, and magazines, as well as current trends, fads, and thinking.

product crossover Promotion of each other's products by two unrelated companies. Fast food restaurants commonly offer toys related to a movie in their children's meals.

product placement The intentional use of a recognizable product within a movie or television program, such as the placement of a particular cereal box on a main character's kitchen table. The purpose is to interest the viewer in the product. The manufacturer of the product often gives money or products in exchange for the placement.

production The end result of the designing, developing, and plans for distribution of media messages.

public service announcement (PSA) An announcement on television or radio for charitable, safety, public interest, or other worthwhile endeavors. They are presented free of charge by broadcasters.

purpose The reason or motivation for a message.

rating The percentage of all television households that are known to be viewing a particular program. For example, a rating of 15 means that 15 percent of all television households were tuned in to a program.

sitcom Situation comedies on television. The format is usually 30 minutes in length, with regular characters and setting. The sitcom airs once a week.

slogan A short phrase that is used to identify a product or group.

soft news The portion of a newspaper or news program that is extraneous or added for human interest. Examples are society or restaurant columns in a newspaper or a celebrity interview during a television news broadcast.

soundbite A small amount of audio or video text that is meant to capture the essence of a speech or document. Length may vary but in general soundbites are from five to 15 seconds.

special effects The technical manipulation of graphics, pictures, and sounds to create an illusion.

statistics The collection, analysis, and interpretation of numbers (data). Statistics are often used to convince people to think, vote, or behave a certain way.

stereotype An oversimplified description based on limited experience. Television programs often use stereotyped characters such as a hillbilly or nosy mother-in-law who are instantly recognizable by viewers.

storyboard A scene-by-scene depiction of a story, including detailed sketches with notes about voice-overs, sound effects, and other media elements that accompany the scenes.

tabloid A term given to weekly newspapers that focus on sensational or bizarre news stories. Tabloids are typically filled with celebrity scoops or human-interest stories, a great deal of photographic matter, and are half the page size of a full-sized newspaper.

target audience The group of viewers toward whom a particular program, movie, commercial, or advertisement is directed.

target marketing Programming or advertising aimed at a specific age, ethnic, income, or otherwise defined group.

MEDIA LITERACY RESOURCES AND ORGANIZATIONS

The following resources were selected from hundreds of books, Web sites, videos, and other materials that might help educators implement the media literacy process.

Books

The Barefoot Book of Heroic Children, Rebecca Hazell, Barefoot Books, 2000.

The Children's Book of Heroes, William J. Bennett, Scholastic, 1997.

Changing the World through Media Education, Rosen, Quesada, and Summers, Fulcrum Publishing, 1998.

Empowering Students With Technology, Alan November, Pearson Professional Development, 2001.

50 American Heroes Every Kid Should Meet, Dennis Denenberg and Lorraine Roscoe, Millbrook Press, 2001.

Getting the Most Out of Teaching with Newspapers, Rebecca Olien, Scholastic Professional Books, 2002.

MEDIA ALERT! 200 Activities to Create Media-Savvy Kids, Sue Lockwood Summers, MEDIA ALERT, 2000.

Stay Tuned: Television's Unforgettable Moments, Joe Garner, Andrews McMeel Publishing, 2002. (includes two CDs and one DVD)

Tales of True Heroism, Paul Dowswell, Usborne Publishing, 1996.

True Tales of Heroes & Heroines, Valerie Marsh, Alleyside Press, 1999.

We Interrupt This Broadcast, Joe Garner, Sourcebooks, MediaFusion, 2002. (Includes two audio CDs)

The Web-Savvy Student: Ten Media Literacy Activities to Help Students Use the Internet Wisely, Betsy Hedberg, Curriculum Adventures, 2001.

Print Resources, Kits, and Guides

Blowing Smoke, The University of Arizona, Rural Health Office, 2001

"The EYE SPY Program," a media literacy coloring book, <www.primett.org>

Famous Faces from TIME, Time For Kids

"Heroes for Today" section in the monthly *Reader's Digest*

Issues and Images from TIME, Time for Kids

Nonfiction Comprehension Test Practice, Time For Kids

"Sitcom Sleuths," a media literacy board game, <www.primett.org>

Test Prep with TIME For Kids, Time for Kids

"Welcome to the Web: An Activity Booklet for Parents and Kids," Educational Programming and Outreach Department, WGBH-TV, Boston, <www.wgbh.org>

Media Literacy Assessment

"Measuring the acquisition of media literacy skills," Hobbs, Renee and Frost, Richard. *Reading Research Quarterly*, Vol. 38, Number 3, July/August/September 2003, pp. 330-355.

Web Sites
Media Literacy Information and Resources

<www.medialiteracy.net>
<www.medialiteracy.com>
<www.ciconline.org/Enrichment/MediaLiteracy>
<www.mediachannel.org/classroom>
<www.primett.org>
<www.MediaAlert.org>

Advertising Lessons

<http://pbskids.org/dontbuyit>
<www.cln.org/themes/media_advert.html>
<http://towerofenglish.com/advertising.html>

News

<www.newseum.org>
<www.timeforkids.com>
<http://teacher.scholastic.com>
<www.educationworld.com/a_curr/curr163.shtml>

Alan November's Web Site

<www.anovember.com>

Teacher Lesson Plan Web Sites

<www.4teachers.org>
<www.lessonplansearch.com>

Electronics & Entertainment Explanations

<www.howstuffworks.com>

Animation

<www.pixar.com>

Making Music, Elementary Level

<http://pbskids.org/dontbuyit/entertainment/makingmusic.html>

Media Literacy Lesson Plans

<www.media-awareness.ca/english/teachers/index.cfm>
<http://discoveryschool.com/lessonplans/health.html>
<www.studentactivities.com>
<www.med.sc.edu:1081/mcreladv.htm>
<www.kqed.org/topics/education/educators/lessons/media-literacy.jsp>
<www.pbs.org/teachersource/media_lit/getting_started.shtm>

Government Documents

<www.ourdocuments.gov>

Political Cartoons

<www.mediaworkshop.org/september11/cartoons.html>
<http://cagle.slate.msn.com/>
<http://orpheus.uscd.edu/speccoll/dspolitic>

Adbusters (for High School and College)

<www.adbusters.org>

Grassroots Taxonomy of Thinking (from Canada)

<www.schoolnet.ca/grassroots/e/project.centre/shared/taxonomy.asp>

Media Literacy Article

"Media Literacy: Yes, It Fits in Math and Science Classrooms"
<www.enc.org/focus/literacy/document.shtm?input=FOC-002081-index>

Media Literacy Integration Ideas
   <www.Ithaca.edu/looksharp/resources/integration>

Carnegie Hero Fund Commission
   <www.carnegiehero.org>

Urban Legends
   <www.snopes.com>
   <http://urbanlegends.about.com/science/urbanlegends>
   <http://HoaxBusters.ciac.org>

Internet Safety and Information
   <www.safekids.com>
   <www.getnetwise.org>

Domain Information
   <www.netsol.com/cgi-bin/whois/whois>
   <www.alltheweb.com>

Web Site Evaluation
   <www.ithaca.edu/library/Training/ICYouSee.html>
   <http://lib.nmsu.edu/instruction/eval.html>
   <www2.widener.edu/Wolfgram-Memorial-Library/webevaluation/perspg
      .htm>
   <www.lib.berkeley.edu/TeachingLib/Guides/Internet/Evaluate.html>
   <www.kathyschrock.com/abceval/index.htm>
   <http://school.discovery.com/schrockguide/eval.html>
   <www.ithaca.edu/looksharp/resources/credibility.html>
   <www.media-awareness.ca/english/special_initiatives/games/joecool_
      joefool/jo_cool_teachers.cfm>

Tobacco Web Sites
   <http://tobaccofreekids.org/adgallery>
   <www.tobaccofreekids.org>
   <www.kickbuttsday.org>
   <www.med.sc.edu:1081/smoking.htm>

Media Literacy Clearing House Sites
   <www.med.sc.edu:1081>
   <www.pbs.org/teachersource/media_lit/related_study.shtm>
   <http://interact.uoregon.edu/MediaLit/mlr/home/index.html>

Assignment Media Literacy: Maryland Project
   <www.msde.state.md.us/assignment_media_lit/home.html>

Media Literacy Online Project
   <http://interact.uoregon.edu/medialit/homepage>

Who Owns the Media?
<www.openairwaves.org>

"Storyworks" Literature Magazine
<http://teacher.scholastic.com/scholasticnews/magazines/storyworks/current
/index.asp>

Media Literacy within the State Standards
<www.med.sc.edu:1081/statelit.htm>
<http://198.17.205.11/compendium/Benchmark.asp?SubjectID=7&
StandardID=10>

McREL National Standards and Benchmarks Compendium
<www.mcrel.org/compendium/browse.asp>

Nielsen Ratings
<http://tv.yahoo.com/Nielsen>

Math in the Media
<www.med.sc.edu:1081/mathinthemedia.htm>

Web Sites for Popular Networks
A&E Network	<www.aetv.com/class>
Biography Channel	<www.aetv.com/class>
BRAVO	<www.bravotv.com/Bravo_in_the_Classroom>
Cable in the Classroom	<www.ciconline.com>
Cable News Network (CNN)	<www.cnnstudentnews.com>
Discovery Channel	<http://discoveryschool.com>
The History Channel	<www.historychannel.com/classroom>
Home & Garden Television	<www.HGTV.com>
Nickelodeon Channel	<www.teachers.nick.com>
WAM!	<www.wamtv.com>
PBS POV Program	<www.pbs.org/pov/classroom.php>

"School House Rock" videos and CDs, including the "School House Rocks the Vote" CD
<www.school-house-rock.com>

"Liberty's Kids," PBS Television Program
<http://pbskids.org/libertyskids>

"How's That Work?" Series
<www.HGTV.com>

Teacher's Guide to Making Student Movies
<http://teacher.scholastic.com/technology/tutor/movie.htm>

Adobe® Sites for Educators
<www.adobe.com/education/digkids/lessons/>
<www.adobe.com/education/webtech/main.html>

Software
Decisions, Decisions 5.0 series: "Violence in the Media," "On the Campaign Trail," "Substance Abuse"
<www.tomsnyder.com>
"Between the Lines" (Grades 8-12, making media software)
<www.tyndal.com>

Videotapes and Guides
From GPN: <http://gpn.unl.edu>
"Beyond the Front Page," set of videos and guide
"Critical Viewing," video and guide
"The Furry News: How to Make a Newspaper," Reading Rainbow video
"TV Planet," video and guide
"TV Confidential," video and guide

"The American Promise" (Free Video and Guide)
<www.farmers.com/FarmComm/AmericanPromise>

Tobacco Control Materials, Centers for Disease Control and Prevention, Office On Smoking and Health, < www.cdc.gov/tobacco/edumat.htm>
"MediaSharp," "Secrets Through the Smoke," "Smoke Screeners"

Media Literacy Organizations
The Alliance for a Media Literate America
<www.amlainfo.org>
The Association for Media Literacy (Canada)
<www.aml.ca>
Center for Media Literacy
<www.medialit.org>
Children Now
<www.childrennow.org>
Consumer Reports for Kids
<www.zillions.org>
Just Think
<www.justthink.org>
MEDIA ALERT!
<www.MediaAlert.org>
Media Awareness Network (Canada)
<www.media-awareness.ca>
National Institute on Media and Family
<www.mediaandthefamily.org>
National Telemedia Council
<www.nationaltelemediacouncil.org>

New Mexico Media Literacy Project
<www.nmmlp.org>
PRIIME TIIME TODAY
<www.primett.org>
Project Look Sharp
<www.ithaca.edu/looksharp>

INDEX

ABOUT THE AUTHOR

Sue Lockwood Summers has been a library media specialist in Colorado elementary schools for more than twenty years. She is the author of *MEDIA ALERT! 200 Activities to Create Media-Savvy Kids* and the co-author of *Changing the World through Media Education.* Sue received her B.A from the State University of New York at Potsdam, New York, and her M.A. from the University of Northern Colorado.

Sue also serves on the Governing Board of PRIIME TIIME TODAY (Parents Responsibly Involved In Media Excellence and Teens Involved In Media Excellence), a non-profit organization in Littleton, Colorado, which sponsors annual media literacy essay and PSA contests. She helped develop a media literacy coloring book and media literacy board game for PTT. She is a former member of the Turner Learning National Faculty.

Sue is an advocate for media literacy and frequently speaks at schools and educational conferences. She writes media literacy curriculum and is the director of MEDIA ALERT! Visit her Web site at <www.MediaAlert.org>

Sue can be contacted at Sue@MediaAlert.org and is always eager to hear from other media literacy enthusiasts.